THE
MEXICANS:
AN INSIDE VIEW OF
A CHANGING SOCIETY

Paula Heusinkveld, Ph.D.

Renaissance Publications
7819 Barkwood Drive
Worthington, OH 43085

Library of Congress Cataloging in Publication Data

Heusinkveld, Paula Rae.
      The Mexicans: An Inside View of a Changing Society
      by Paula R. Heusinkveld
  p. cm.
  ISBN 0-936645-09-1
  Includes bibliographical references

  1. Mexico--Social life and customs
  2. Mexico.

    I. Title.

  F1210.H48   1993
  973.--dc20

                   91-61380
                     CIP

Cover Design by Brad Egnor

Printed in the United States of America
10 9 8 7 6 5 4 3 2 1

Prof. Valade   *Spring 96*

Table of Contents

Preface

When I was growing up in a small Midwestern town, Mexico seemed faraway and exotic. It was the land of sombreros and mustachioed guitarists, of mysterious temples and sun-drenched beaches. This alluring land seemed to bear no relation to the more sobering image presented in United States newspaper headlines—the Mexico of poverty, overpopulation, and illegal immigration.

Neither the idealized images of travel brochures nor the negative stereotypes of economic despair do justice to our closest neighbor to the south. Mexico is fascinating, complex, and—for the unsuspecting visitor—potentially addictive. Little did I know on my first visit there nearly thirty years ago that Mexico would become an obsession, a lifetime adventure, drawing me back again and again.

Volumes have been written on Mexican culture, yet misunderstandings between Mexicans and Anglo-Americans persist. Despite our common border of nearly two thousand miles, our histories and cultural traditions divide us. Perhaps nowhere in the world does a national border separate two such different countries. In this last decade of the twentieth century, as the United States and Mexico negotiate to expand trade relations, the need for mutual understanding is more compelling than ever.

This need, coupled with my own lifelong endeavor to know the Mexicans, has brought into being this book, a concise overview of Mexican culture. *The Mexicans* considers not only time-honored traditions and values, but also those attitudes and behaviors that are changing in response to Mexico's rapid modernization and increasing interdependence with the United States. I hope that the insights offered here will help to create greater understanding and appreciation of the Mexican people. With greater awareness of what we have in common and what makes us different, we can hope to become better neighbors.

Acknowledgements

I would like to express my gratitude to Deborah Hill of Renaissance Publications for proposing this project to me and encouraging me throughout. Without her planting the seed, this book would never have been written. I am also grateful to my department head, Judith M. Melton, my dean, Robert Waller of the College of Liberal Arts, and the administration of Clemson University for granting me the six-month sabbatical in spring 1991, which allowed me the necessary time to devote to writing this book.

Many friends and associates gave much needed support and encouragement through the various phases of this book. Chuck Harty patiently helped me to work through my phobia of personal computers and convinced me that I could undertake a project of this scope.

Rufina Parissi de Mendoza of Xalapa, in the state of Veracruz, Mexico, housed and mothered me for five months in early 1991 and for one month in the summer of 1992, and offered many cultural insights. Marcela, Doriam, Reina, and Carmen of her household patiently answered my innumerable questions about contemporary Mexican culture.

Dr. Andree Fleming-Holland, Barbara de Gomez, and Patricia Reidy provided invaluable observations based on years of living as Americans in Mexico, while Magno Villa, Teresa Barrera and Leticia Loria de Montiel critiqued portions of the manuscript from a Mexican perspective. Manuel Alarcon Camarillo and his staff at the Institute of Practical Computing in Xalapa regularly printed copies of various chapters and offered me computer tips, as well as moral support. A special thank-you to Jorge Medina Morales and to all my friends in Xalapa, whose ongoing generosity and hospitality provided me with an infinite variety of experiences that sharpened my understanding of changing Mexican life-styles and values.

Friends who helped to refine portions of the manuscript after my return to the United States include M. E. Anderson, Dixie Goswami, Harriet Heusinkveld, Craig Johnson, and Priscilla Phillips. Special thanks to Susan Lovitt for her expert editing of the entire manuscript. Thanks also to Todd Mohler, who drew the maps, to reference librarian Lisa Ridenour, who offered invaluable assistance with the appendix, and to Jackie Worley and Cary Wilkins for their careful proofreading.

Finally, I would like to express my gratitude to the dozens of students who have traveled with me to Mexico on various study programs over the past twenty years. Their observations, questions, and thoughtful independent studies have contributed immeasurably to my own knowledge of Mexican culture.

Most especially, a loving thank-you to my mother, Emma Lou Heusinkveld, and my late father, George R. Heusinkveld, who through the years always encouraged me to travel and explore new places. Without that impetus, the impressions, observations, and cross-cultural insights contained in this volume would never have been possible.

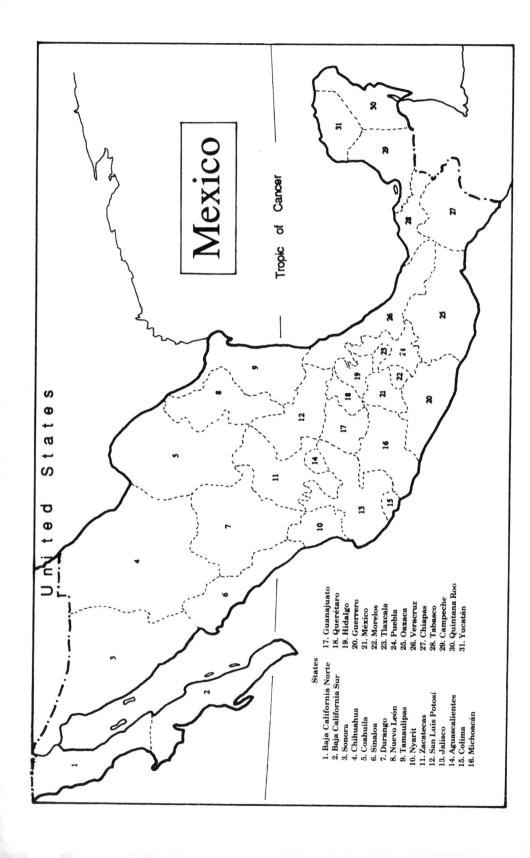

Mexico

Tropic of Cancer

United States

States

1. Baja California Norte
2. Baja California Sur
3. Sonora
4. Chihuahua
5. Coahuila
6. Sinaloa
7. Durango
8. Nuevo León
9. Tamaulipas
10. Nayarit
11. Zacatecas
12. San Luis Potosí
13. Jalisco
14. Aguascalientes
15. Colima
16. Michoacán
17. Guanajuato
18. Querétaro
19. Hidalgo
20. Guerrero
21. México
22. Morelos
23. Tlaxcala
24. Puebla
25. Oaxaca
26. Veracruz
27. Chiapas
28. Tabasco
29. Campeche
30. Quintana Roo
31. Yucatán

Introduction

Things Are Not Always What They Seem

José Luis Ibarra, a successful Mexican businessman who had just arrived in the United States, was given an appointment from 4:00 to 5:00 with Fred Lawson, an important potential contact. Mr. Ibarra arrived at 4:45, excited and ready to do business. Great were his disappointment and bewilderment when he was received coldly and dismissed fifteen minutes later.

What had gone wrong? Mr. Ibarra had been impeccably dressed and had shown perfect manners. He had arrived at Mr. Lawson's office exactly at the time indicated—or had he?

From Mr. Lawson's perspective, Ibarra had arrived inexcusably late, almost at the end of the appointment. Mr. Ibarra, however, had understood that he had a comfortable one-hour window of time for his arrival and that the meeting would be open-ended. In fact, Mr. Ibarra had set aside the entire evening for this important meeting. He had assumed that the meeting would follow a leisurely pace, since building the kind of trust necessary to do business takes time. Furthermore, Mr. Ibarra never imagined that his associate would state a specific hour for the interview to end, since this would violate Mexican rules of hospitality. How could a guest be welcome for only a precisely prescribed amount of time?

Mr. Ibarra left the office convinced that the United States businessman was rude, cold, and impatient. Mr. Lawson concluded that the Mexican was irresponsible and unprofessional. Two well-meaning gentlemen lost an opportunity to do business together because of a simple cultural misunderstanding. Unfortunately, their encounter only reinforced negative stereotypes that each man held of the other's culture.

Mexican Presence in the United States

Like many people in the United States, Mr. Lawson has much to learn about Mexican people and culture. Certainly, he *thought* he knew something about the Mexican way of life. Because of the growing Mexican presence in the United States, images of Mexican culture abound: supermarket shelves from coast to coast display tortilla shells and refried beans, and Mexican restaurants offer tacos, enchiladas, and chiles rellenos to an enthusiastic clientele.

Furthermore, Mexican-Americans increasingly are making their presence known in business, entertainment, and politics. In cities throughout the southwestern United States, advertisers address the Mexican-American market, and television and radio stations offer programming in Spanish, including Mexican soap operas. At the ballot box, Mexican-Americans, often called Chicanos, have influenced both local and state elections.

Reasons for Negative Stereotypes

Unfortunately, physical proximity does not always lead to understanding. Through the years, a variety of negative stereotypes have severely impeded a harmonious relationship with our southern neighbors.

To begin with, Hollywood has perpetuated misleading stereotypes of Mexicans. Mexico City, a sprawling metropolis of over twenty million people, bears no more resemblance to the Hollywood land of siestas under the cactus than Los Angeles and San Francisco resemble the Western movie sets of yesteryear. Nevertheless, because of Americans' lack of familiarity with Mexico, the Hollywood image persists.

Further and more damaging misunderstandings result from the presence of many itinerant Mexican-American farm workers in the United States. These migrants, often lacking formal education, are those who were least able to make their way in their own country. Americans of European descent are apt to judge these people with disdain for their lack of material success, while overlooking their warmth, good humor, and generosity. Even worse, some Anglo-Americans[1] base their opinion of all Mexicans on this atypical sample

---

[1]Unfortunately, there is no convenient single adjective such as *United Statesian* to refer to people from the United States. The word *American* can technically refer to anyone from North, Central, or South America. The term *North American,* while more specific, could refer to anyone from Canada, the United States, or Mexico. To refer to people from the United States as *Anglo-Americans* is also inexact, since this term excludes most minority and immigrant groups.

This book uses the term *American* to refer to citizens of the United States and *Anglo-American* for people of the dominant culture of the United States, particularly in contrast to Mexicans and Mexican-Americans.

group, seemingly unaware that Mexican doctors, lawyers, and businessmen and women are living financially successful lives south of the border and in the United States.

Another cause for misunderstanding is that many official documents in the United States classify all Hispanics together, giving the impression that these peoples are all alike. While Hispanics from various countries do share many cultural values, each national group is unique. The geography, history, political system, and ethnic composition of Mexico are entirely different from those of Cuba, Puerto Rico, or Argentina, to say nothing of Spain. Furthermore, Mexicans have their own national heroes, holidays, folklore, and culinary traditions.

Mexican border cities have also contributed to erroneous stereotypes. Border cities tend to attract those Mexicans who are economically desperate and eager to cross into the United States. With a high rate of poverty, some of these cities are among the least attractive and most crime-ridden in Mexico. Many Anglo-Americans mistakenly assume that such cities must be typical. Ironically, middle-class Mexicans who live comfortably and safely much farther south believe that the rough character of some border towns is due to their proximity to the United States, a country known for its high rate of violent crimes!

The Mexican cities most visited by people from the United States—resorts such as Cancún, Acapulco, and Puerto Vallarta—are not typical either. These beach resorts present an idealized but superficial view of Mexico: a life of perpetual leisure characterized by tequila, sunshine, and white sand beaches.

More Cultural Misunderstandings

The stereotypes and the misunderstandings continue. In the workplace, in schools, and in social situations, well-meaning people from both sides of the border misinterpret the actions of others due to cultural differences.

Frank Johnson could not hide his irritation over the absence of his new Mexican-American employee, Rosa Gutiérrez. "I can't believe Rosa would dare to miss a full day's work to go to a kid's birthday party. She knew we had to finish that contract today. Yet she cut out to go to some niece's birthday party—was it fourteen years old, or fifteen? I guess Rosa must not take this job very seriously!"

In the meantime, Rosa was distressed by her boss's utter lack of sensitivity to her family obligations. Rosa was not attending an ordinary birthday party, but rather a *quinceaños*, a very special occasion in the life of a Mexican girl. The *quinceaños* (literally fifteen years) is a Mexican girl's introduction into society, an elegant coming-out party similar to a debutante ball. Usually the birthday is celebrated with a Catholic mass, followed by a large reception and dance. Relatives drive for hundreds of miles to attend a *quinceaños*. The family would have been surprised and hurt if Rosa had failed to appear at such an important event in the life of her niece, especially since family obligations usually take top priority in Mexican culture.

In an elementary school in Chicago, Mrs. Patterson took Manolito Gómez into the principal's office. "I think Manolito is hiding something from me," she explained. "He refuses to look me in the eye when I speak to him. I don't trust him."

Poor Manolito was mystified as to why his teacher was angry. By casting his eyes downward, he was simply showing respect to his teacher. Direct eye contact with an authority figure such as a teacher is not the norm in Mexico, especially for young children; in fact, in some cases eye contact could be interpreted as insolence. Manolito left the principal's office convinced that his teacher simply didn't like Mexicans.

In a small Midwestern town, Joan and Larry fretted that their Mexican exchange student, Alberto, was not fitting in with the family. "Our own kids all pitch in and help around the house," said Joan. "But Alberto won't lift a finger. He seems to expect us to wait on him hand and foot. He won't even get his own glass of water. He must just be lazy."

In fact, Alberto had impeccable manners and knew exactly how guests should behave—in his own culture. In Mexico, the roles of host and guest are different; the host and hostess take full responsibility for the well-being of their guests. A guest at a Mexican party would not normally offer to serve himself a drink, as this might imply that the host was not being sufficiently generous or attentive. Furthermore, most middle- and upper-class families in Mexico employ maids to assist with household chores. Teenage children, especially sons, would almost never be expected to do housework.

Frank Johnson, Mrs. Patterson, and Joan all arrived at conclusions about Mexicans based on their own cultural assumptions. They all misinterpreted the actions of their Mexican associates.

Clearly, we have much to learn about the way Mexicans think and behave. Learning about the customs, attitudes, and values of another culture is an ongoing, fascinating process that leads to deeper mutual understanding. With over twelve million documented Mexicans and Mexican-Americans in the United States today and the number rapidly growing, it is well worth our while to learn more about our Mexican neighbors.

A Mestizo Nation

The Blending of Two Cultures

Whenever modern Mexicans talk about the historical origins of their country, they are apt to contradict themselves. Did those cruel Spaniards who first arrived on Mexican shores in 1519 come to invade and conquer "us"? Or did "we" bring civilization to those poor heathen Indians?

Invariably, Mexicans resist referring to "we" and "they" in discussions of the Spanish conquest. Simply, the Spaniards conquered the Indians. The Mexicans of today are a fusion of both, members of a blended race—Spanish and Meso-American Indian—whose name is *mestizo* (literally, mixed). Racially and culturally, the blend is more complete in Mexico than anywhere else in Latin America.

Most of the formal structures of Mexican society are the heritage of the conquering Spanish. These include the predominant Catholic religion, the Spanish language, governmental structures, the educational and legal systems, and domestic and public architecture. On the other hand, many aspects of daily life—corn tortillas and black beans, handicrafts, typical dress, folklore, legends, and much of Mexican music and dance—reflect Mexico's Indian heritage.

Attitudes and values of Mexicans today also reflect the inextricable blend of Hispanic and Indian cultures. For example, the Mexicans' strong sense of dignity and personal honor is part of the Spanish heritage. From the indigenous culture comes Mexico's characteristic fatalism, a stoic acceptance of things as they are. Some of Mexico's most deeply held values are the inheritance of both Hispanic and Indian cultures: distinct gender roles, male dominance, and devotion to family.

Any attempt by Mexicans to explain who they are must take into account both parts of their cultural heritage. From the high desert country of Mexico's northwest to the lush tropical coasts in the south, Hispanic and indigenous traditions have blended together in myriad ways to produce the rich cultural mosaic that is Mexico today.

Where is the "Typical" Mexican?

To describe a typical Mexican is a challenge, inasmuch as the word *Mexican* includes almost as many different types of people as the words *United States citizen*. Life-styles and values of Mexico's eighty million people vary widely according to region, socioeconomic class, urban/rural setting, and ethnic group.

Mexicans may be light-skinned, blond mestizos in suit and tie or cinnamon-colored Indians in native dress. They may be sophisticated urbanites or simple peasants in a remote mountain valley. Mexicans may dwell in windswept high plateaus or tropical port cities. They may be fabulously rich or distressingly poor. Within every city and every social stratum, one finds some families who cling to traditional values and others who welcome change.

More than twenty million people, about one quarter of all Mexicans, live in Mexico City, which vies with Tokyo for the dubious honor of being the largest city in the world. Like New Yorkers, the inhabitants of Mexico City are streetwise, cosmopolitan, and usually in a hurry. They speak often about "getting away to the provinces" for some peace and quiet, but they never seem to get around to it, except for the traditional Easter exodus to the beaches. On some level, they thrive on the hustle and bustle. The tastes, fashions, and values of people in México D.F. (Distrito Federal, or Federal District) reflect the constant contact with visitors from all over the world.

Outside the capital, regional variations in geography and climate contribute to striking differences in personality and life-styles. Natives of the tropical Gulf port of Veracruz (often called *jarochos*), are famous for their ebullient, carefree, hospitable nature. By contrast, inhabitants of the interior, semidesert city of San Luis Potosí are reputed to be more taciturn and introspective.

Other variations in lifestyle and attitude reflect the diverse histories of individual Mexican cities. In Taxco and Guanajuato, colonial silver-mining cities with cobblestone streets, visitors cannot help but direct their thoughts toward the past. Mexican inhabitants of these historic places thrive on their cities' rich traditions. On the other hand, in fast-growing border towns with booming *maquiladora* industries (assembly plants), the orientation is toward the future. The same applies to new resorts such as Cancún, a city which was created in the early 1970s to promote international tourism. Here, there is no past; a sense of the transitory prevails.

Ethnic variations account for still other regional contrasts; areas with a heavy Indian population have a different "feel." Mérida, in the state of Yucatán, for example, reflects the Mayan heritage of the area in its food, dress, music, and regional dances. Oaxaca, located in the heart of what was formerly the Zapotec/Mixtec civilization, is famous for its pottery, weavings, and other indigenous crafts. Cities in the desert of northwest Mexico reflect the Yaqui Indian culture in dress, crafts, and dances. In all, ethnographers list around fifty different indigenous groups in Mexico today, with as many different Indian languages.[1]

In Search of Historical Role Models

More than in most other Latin American countries, Mexicans have glorified their Indian past. When Mexicans look for historical role models, they are infinitely more likely to turn to Cuauhtémoc, the last Aztec emperor, than to Hernán Cortés, the Spanish conquistador. Statues to Cuauhtémoc abound; streets, boulevards, schools, neighborhoods, and babies bear his name. By contrast, there are almost no statues of Cortés, and one would be hard pressed to find his name anywhere in Mexico except in the history books.

Most Mexicans have ambivalent feelings about their indigenous heritage. While they point with justifiable pride to the monumental temples and exquisite artifacts of Mexico's Indian past, many have not come to terms with Mexico's Indian present. The word *indio* (Indian) is often derogatory, implying backwardness and social naïveté. Many middle- and upper-class mothers rejoice when they give birth to blond children and express displeasure when their older children date dark-skinned sweethearts. This seems especially true in regions with large Indian populations.

As in many other Hispanic countries, the word *indio* in Mexico has more to do with culture than race. The small minority known today as *indios* or *indígenas* (natives) are those who continue to live in their communities, wear traditional dress, and speak indigenous languages. If a pure-blooded indigenous couple were to move to the city and adopt Western dress and lifestyle, their children would probably be considered mestizos.

---

[1]The exact number of Indian groups varies slightly, according to the source. The National Institute of Anthropology and History (INAH) reports fifty-four indigenous cultures in Mexico today. For detailed descriptions and photographs of forty-six different indigenous groups, see Lucio Mendieta y Núñez, *México Indígena* (Mexico, D.F.: Editorial Porrúa, 1986

Urban/Rural Contrasts

Like other Indians throughout the Americas, the peoples of pre-Columbian Mexico thought of human beings as part of nature, with the responsibility to honor and protect the natural world. The conquering Spaniards, on the other hand, thought of cities as the repositories of civilization and had little regard for life in the country. This latter attitude has prevailed until now; it affects the way Mexicans think of life in the cities and the country.

Middle- and upper-class Mexicans almost invariably would prefer to live in the cities, which offer technology, education, consumer goods, financial services, professional opportunities, communication networks, and other services unavailable in many small towns or rural areas. With economic and political power concentrated in the cities, rural development has often been a low priority in public policy. Consequently, the contrast between the lifestyle of city and country remains much greater in Mexico than in the United States.

Life in the country lacks many modern amenities and tends to be associated with the Indian way of life. In many regions, the word *campesino* (literally, person from the country) may be used to avoid the derogatory word *indio*. The phrase *viene del campo* (he comes from the country) often implies ignorance and naïveté about modern ways.

The smaller the town, the more traditional the lifestyle. In the remotest areas, in mountain communities inaccessible by road, life continues as it has for centuries. In some rural areas, people still live by subsistence agriculture, with no electricity, running water, or plumbing.

Thus, Mexicans migrate to the cities by the hundreds of thousands in search of a better life. For those who are fortunate, the cities offer the opportunity for a higher standard of living. However, all too many migrants join the urban poor in their struggle to eke out a marginal daily existence.

Role Models for the Future

If Mexicans turn to their indigenous past for historical role models, they are apt to look to the United States for models for the future. Generally, the larger the city, the greater is the influence of United States products and life-styles. Urban Mexicans of the upper and upper-middle classes may enjoy all the benefits of modern technology including personal computers, VCRs, satellite dishes, compact disc players, and microwave ovens.

Also in evidence in the larger cities are United States mores and values, including the concepts of working for success, self-sufficiency, and independence for women. More Mexican women are working every day, and more young people are living independently from their parents.

Despite their imitation of some elements of United States culture, most Mexicans have a love/hate relationship with their powerful neighbors to the north. They generally admire and covet American technology and material prosperity, as well as American fashions, sports heroes, music, television programs, movies, and all other forms of popular culture. At the same time, Mexicans resent the conspicuous wealth and the imperiousness of their northern neighbors. Porfirio Díaz, the dictatorial president of Mexico from 1877 until the Mexican Revolution in 1910, once lamented, "Poor Mexico—so far from God and so close to the United States!"

In the view of most Mexicans today, the pervasive influence of United States culture is a mixed blessing. For example, as urban women become more self-sufficient, divorce rates gradually rise. Formerly relaxing lunch hours become shorter as ambitious urban professionals hurry back to work.

What is "Mexican" Culture?

Somewhere in between the two extremes of the isolated rural Indian and the success-driven urban professional lie the vast majority of Mexicans. Their patterns of daily living, attitudes, mores, and values comprise Mexico's dominant mestizo culture. This book focuses not on curious regional or ethnic variations, but rather on those commonalities of attitudes and behaviors that seem to transcend social class, ethnic heritage, and regional differences throughout Mexico. Subsequent chapters offer insights on those commonalities that together distinguish the majority of Mexicans from people of other cultures, especially Anglo-Americans.

The Family

Stability in the Midst of Change

Despite rapidly changing mores and values during the past two decades, the family remains the most enduring of all Mexican institutions. In the larger cities, a higher standard of living and increased contact with the United States are significantly altering traditional family structure and values. Yet from the most provincial village to the bustling capital, from the most conservative family to the most liberal, the family continues to provide each Mexican with a measure of moral and emotional support throughout life, from cradle to grave.

On the surface, the familial structure remains largely unchanged. For Mexicans, the word *familia* has always included far more than mother, father, sons, and daughters. In fact, the Spanish language has no convenient way to express the idea of "extended family." *Familia* assumes the inclusion of grandparents, uncles, aunts, nieces and nephews, cousins, and in-laws.

The Most Reliable Support System

In a society where the government is perceived as corrupt and trust is difficult to obtain, the broad network of relatives called *familia* is crucial. To an even greater degree than in some other Hispanic countries, Mexicans turn first to family in times of need. The extended family provides a safety net to sustain and support an individual in time of crisis, be it financial, emotional, medical, or legal in nature.[1] Even as the population becomes more mobile, most Mexicans still find their most reliable and enduring support system within the family.

---

[1] See Alan Riding, *Distant Neighbors: A Portrait of the Mexicans,* (New York: Alfred A. Knopf, 1985), 238-253.

Intergenerational Family Gatherings

The family also provides a core of social relations; Mexicans generally gather with the extended family for holidays, anniversaries, saint's days, and birthdays. Family gatherings still take priority over most other commitments. A Mexican businessman might postpone an important meeting in order to attend the birthday party of a niece or nephew. A Mexican teenager would probably be expected to attend a grandparent's birthday party, even if it conflicted with an outing with other teenagers.

These intergenerational festivities result in a comfortable mingling between young and old. Mexican children are socialized from the cradle to interact with people of all ages. At a typical family gathering, a smiling baby might be passed from the hands of one doting relative to another. At the same time, the elderly enjoy the affection and respect of younger family members.

The care of young children is frequently entrusted to grandparents or other relatives. In fact, until recently, many Mexicans found that they almost never needed to go beyond the family to find a baby-sitter. Now, as grown sons and daughters migrate to larger cities, the concept of paid baby-sitters is becoming more accepted.

Changing Values for Teens and Young Adults

As Mexican children grow older, they are generally more closely supervised in their behavior than their American counterparts. Whereas American teenagers speak of having *privileges* (to stay out late, for example), Mexican teenagers receive *permiso* (permission) to go out. These different words reflect somewhat different attitudes: most young Mexicans do not take for granted the right to stay out late, or even to go out at all. Even so, behavior patterns are liberalizing every day. Parents complain that their teenage children are bringing home too many modern ideas; teens accuse their parents of being old-fashioned.

For older teens in the cities, the most popular gathering places are the discotheques. With their nearly deafening music and pulsating strobe lights, these cavernous centers of entertainment attract Mexican young people like a magnet.

By appealing to peer pressure, a majority of Mexican teens aged fifteen or sixteen and older eventually get parental permission to go to the disco. Although the legal drinking age is eighteen years, enforcement of this law is so lax as to be almost nonexistent. Nevertheless, there is almost no drunkenness. Also popular are video bars, where young people can have a snack and watch videos.

As teenagers grow into young adults, rapidly changing values become even more apparent. On the surface, ties remain strong between young Mexican adults and their parents. Most unmarried Mexicans continue to live with their parents and sleep at home every night until they are married. This applies even to unmarried children in their late twenties or thirties. This is vastly different from the situation in the United States, where a youth is strongly encouraged to go away to college or get out on his own.

The fact that most unmarried Mexican adults continue to live under the parental roof has much more to do with economics than behavioral mores; separate living quarters for grown unmarried sons and daughters are simply not economically feasible for many families. Besides, parents feel responsible to provide for their children until the latter are well established.

The degree of independence possible for young adults living at home has increased dramatically in recent years, especially for males. A twenty-five-year-old son with a room in his parents' home might have complete independence to come and go as he pleases, including staying out all night. An unmarried adult daughter living at home with her parents, by contrast, is still subject to parental supervision and may even have a curfew.

The idea of young people setting up their own apartments is gradually becoming more accepted in Mexico, though it is still the exception rather than the rule. A single young man who sets up his own apartment in the same city where his parents live is apt to be regarded somewhat negatively. Why would he spend all that money to have his own space, when he could live at home, eat well, have his laundry done, and generally have all his material needs taken care of? People might assume either that the young man had quarreled with his father, or that he must be entertaining female guests or otherwise engaging in reproachable behavior. According to traditional thinking, a prudent young Mexican man would do better to find a job and save money by living with his parents until he was ready to get married.

Independence from one's parents is even more difficult to obtain for a single young woman. If a young Mexican woman were to rent an apartment in the same city as her parents, she would risk acquiring a bad reputation. Even if she went to another city to pursue university studies or to work, she would be expected to live with relatives if at all possible, or at least with a respectable family. As more young Mexicans study far from their hometowns in cities where housing is scarce, the concept of shared, single-six student apartments is gradually becoming more accepted. However, living with a respectable family remains the ideal, especially for women.

These values and others are gradually giving way to more "modern" ideas. Premarital sex, while still generally taboo for teenagers, is gradually becoming more accepted among young adults. An adult unmarried daughter who continues to live under the parental roof may find ingenious ways to meet discreetly with her romantic partner. A young couple's Saturday shopping trip to a nearby city may facilitate an afternoon tryst in a hotel room far from parental vigilance. An older bachelor friend may provide an apartment where young couples can meet.

Most Mexican young people would not dream of flaunting their behavior to challenge or shock their parents. Respect for one's parents continues to be valued more highly than personal independence. Thus, as sexual mores and behavior gradually change, discretion remains of utmost importance. The smaller the town, the greater the attention paid to discretion and the appearance of propriety. Young middle-class Mexicans are so discreet that an outsider may not initially realize just how much their behavior has changed in the past decade or two.

Parents are also changing their attitudes. Middle- and upper-class Mexican women now dare to speak openly of situations that were previously unmentionable: unwed teenage mothers, young couples living together, and pregnant brides. In the larger cities, traditional values are eroding most rapidly. In the provinces, behavior is changing, too, though here the upper and middle classes still tend to worry about the *¿qué dirán?* (what will everyone think?).

It should be noted that in the *clases populares* (lower classes), the idea of couples living together has always been taken more for granted. Concern for traditional morality and propriety has generally been more the domain of the middle and upper-middle classes.

Keeping in Touch After Marriage

Even after Mexicans marry, the parents still remain in close touch with the newlyweds. Because the role of *madre* (mother) is central to the identity of so many Mexican women, it may indeed be difficult for the mother to let go once her children are grown and married. Furthermore, since independence in young adults is not encouraged, the mother may have trouble believing that her children can actually fend for themselves.

There are many jokes in Mexico about the meddling *suegra* (mother-in-law). The mother of the groom has an especially bad reputation. It is often difficult for a new daughter-in-law to live up to her mother-in-law's standards of caring for the latter's precious son.

In the past, many Mexicans continued to live right next to their parents after they were grown and married. Even today, some traditional families choose to live in a sort of family compound, with married children and grandchildren living on properties adjacent to the parental home.

While this arrangement is no longer common, most Mexican adults still maintain close contact with their parents, living in the same city when possible. Many married daughters maintain daily contact with their mothers, if only by phone. Family get-togethers on Sundays as well as on all holidays are frequent.

Godparents

In a rapidly changing society, one tradition remains solid and unchanged—that of *padrinos* (godparents). When a baby is born, the new parents choose a *padrino* (godfather) and a *madrina* (godmother) for their child. Usually these are a married couple, typically close friends or relatives of the new parents. Since the godparents are named during the Catholic sacrament of baptism, this obligation is moral rather than legal, yet it is a solemn oath that is taken most seriously. The godparents reinforce and fortify the family support system; in case of the death of the parents, the godparents ideally become the child's guardians. Sometimes a rich or well-known member of the community may be named as godparent. In these cases, the *padrinos* do not comply with traditional obligations, but rather use their influence to place the godchild in a favorable work situation when the time comes.

Traditionally, the mother and godmother become *comadres* (literally, co-mothers), and the two men become *compadres* (co-fathers). The relationship of *comadre* or *compadre* is one of the very closest bonds possible. One cannot choose one's family, but one can choose one's *compadres,* those very special friends who become part of the family. Often the relationship is reciprocal; for example, Señora López may be the godmother of the son of Señora Rodríguez, and vice versa. In this case the bond is even stronger, and this close, special relationship lasts for life.

Nurturing the Elderly, Burying the Dead

When aging relatives are no longer able to care for themselves, they most often live with their children, or in some cases with a niece or nephew. Private nursing homes are exorbitantly expensive for most Mexicans; public facilities, crowded and understaffed, have not been considered a viable option by most families until very recently.

As in most cultures of the world, a death draws a family together. By Mexican law, a person must be buried within twenty-four hours after death. News of a death spreads quickly, and members of the extended family drop whatever they are doing to be with the family for the *velorio* (wake). *Compadres,* intimate friends, and other family members stay with the body of the deceased throughout the night, until the funeral service and burial the following day.

Family members who live in other cities make every effort to arrive in time for the burial, even if it means driving all night. In the words of one Mexican who gave up a long-planned trip to the beach to attend a funeral, "It is a moral obligation to attend my cousin's burial; I could not conceive of doing otherwise."

Thus, from infancy to death, the family remains at the core of a Mexican's existence. Nothing matters more to a Mexican than a close, harmonious family life. And in the broad network of relatives that a family provides, the Mexican continues to find his most reliable and enduring support system in an uncertain, seemingly hostile world.

Language

How Language Reflects Cultural Values

In every culture in the world, people use language to describe their life experience, to articulate their needs, to express their deepest feelings. Each language reflects faithfully the culture that produced it, with its own particular world view and values. Even those people who are fluent in several languages tend to resort to their native language in moments of crisis or intense emotion—to curse, to express joy, to pray. For thousands of Mexicans living in the United States, language remains the strongest link with their native culture.

The Art of Conversation

The Spanish language has two forms of address, the formal *usted* and the familiar *tú*. Like other Hispanics, Mexicans use *usted* to address strangers and authority figures. But most Mexicans feel more at home once they have lapsed into the familiar *tú*. Mexicans tend to use the *tú* forms more than in some other Hispanic countries. In many situations, the *usted* forms serve to maintain distance and formality between two speakers, while the use of *tú* establishes a warm camaraderie. When two Mexicans meet for the first time, the one who is older or of higher standing may extend the invitation to *tutear* (to speak using the familiar *tú* forms). Once this has happened, the conversation instantly becomes more relaxed.

Just as Mexicans seem to have an innate sense for the appropriate social register (*tú* versus *usted*), they know which topics are best avoided. As in other cultures, some topics are taboo for conversation. Mexicans generally avoid discussion of income, salaries, or investments, except with intimate friends. If a Mexican made a windfall on a land speculation, he would almost surely keep this information to himself.

On the other hand, Mexicans are more likely than Anglos to express their inner beliefs, feelings, and emotions. Whereas Anglos may avoid controversial topics because they might disrupt a pleasant gathering, Mexicans enjoy exposing different views to generate a lively discussion. The ability to express one's views with passion and eloquence is admired by all.

Mexicans love to talk; conversation with friends is a favorite pastime. When Mexicans practice the art of conversation, they become totally engaged. In the course of their discussion, they may gesticulate, talk rapidly and excitedly, interrupt each other, and even raise their voices. Anglos listening to Mexicans discuss a controversial issue might mistakenly think they were angry, when in fact they were simply having a good time.

Flowery Compliments, Colorful Insults

Like most other Hispanics, Mexicans enjoy colorful language. Song lyrics in Mexico are infinitely more poetic than those in the United States. Written invitations and business letters are more flowery and elaborate, and speeches and public addresses are more bombastic. American prose may seem dry and abrupt by comparison.

Both compliments and insults are more imaginative and spicier than in English. The *piropo* is that colorful compliment that a Mexican man calls out to a woman as she walks down the street. Depending on the tone of voice, the words chosen, and the context, these *piropos* can range from innocuous compliments to vulgar insinuations. Smart Mexican women ignore a *piropo* and keep walking.

Mexicans also have a rich vocabulary of swear words and use them liberally, probably more often than in most other Hispanic countries. However, profanity is generally reserved for men. A word that sounds mildly provocative when spoken by a man often sounds vulgar on the lips of a woman. Well-bred Mexican women avoid swearing in mixed company. Females from the United States who visit Mexico should realize that for a woman, swearing in Spanish is culturally inappropriate and may give an impression of vulgarity.

Octavio Paz wrote a famous essay on the very profane and uniquely Mexican verb *chingar* (fuck).[1] Mexicans have made this most powerful word into virtually every part of speech. Someone who violates (literally, rapes) another is a *chingón*; the victim who is

---

[1] Octavio Paz, *The Labyrinth of Solitude: Life and Thought in Mexico,* trans. Lysander Kemp (New York: Grove Press, 1961), 73-88.

violated is *chingado*. In a sense, all Mexicans feel they have been violated, or abused, by history. Mexico began as a country with the rape or violation of the indigenous cultures by the Spanish invaders. Thus, variants of the word *chingar* divide Mexicans into the violators (*chingones*) and the violated (*chingados*).

The insults that raise a Mexican man's blood pressure fastest are those that impinge on the honor of his mother. Insults about one's mother are so well known that the mere words *tu madre* (literally, your mother) are offensive by implication. When a Mexican wants to ask a friend about his mother, he tries to use the word *mamá* (mom) in order to avoid saying *tu madre*. Ironically, an intimate term of endearment for a woman—usually a sexual partner—is *mamacita* (literally, little mother). A woman might call her male partner *papito* or *papi* (little father).

Invoking God's Name—Past, Present, and Future

As in other Hispanic countries, it is perfectly acceptable to use religious words, such as *Dios* (God), *Jesús*, and *Santa María* (Holy Mary) to express surprise or alarm. These words are not considered blasphemous; they invoke God, Jesus, and Mary in an absolutely respectable way. The most appropriate translation for *Dios mío* (literally, my God) would be "Good heavens" or "Gracious." Well-bred Mexican women tend to use these respectable religious words instead of profanity.

The importance of religion in Hispanic culture is evident by constant references to *Dios* in daily conversation. When something bad happens, Mexicans are apt to say, <<*Así lo quiso Dios*>> ("It was God's will"). This phrase could refer to an unavoidable tragedy, such as an accidental death, or to a personal failure, such as losing one's job. And when something good happens, Mexicans are apt to say, <<*Gracias a Dios*>> ("Thanks be to God"). This phrase is used even when the individual might take credit for a personal triumph, such as a college graduation or professional promotion.

<<*Si Dios quiere*>> ("God willing") is a phrase added almost automatically when Mexicans are discussing future plans. This phrase is so common that for many it has become purely a linguistic formula.

Using the Language to Blame Fate

Most Mexicans believe that things happen to people, instead of babies names from indigenous Mexican languages. Some popular names include Cuauhtémoc, after the last Aztec emperor, or names that come from nature, for example, Janik (rain) or Xochitl (flower). In some cases, the parents' decision to give their baby an Indian name may indicate a pro-indigenous political stance, or a subtle protest against the cultural dominance of the Catholic Church.

Many Spanish names have common nicknames. Even when the nicknames bear little resemblance to the given name, everyone recognizes what they mean, like Bob for Robert in English. Some of the most common nicknames for men include Pepe for José, Pancho or Paco for Francisco, Lalo for Eduardo, Memo for Guillermo, Beto for Alberto or Roberto, and Chucho or Chuy for Jesús. Some common nicknames for women include *Lupe* for *Guadalupe*, *Lola* for *Dolores*, *Malena* and *Magda* for *Magdalena*, *Coco* for *Socorro*, and *Conchita* for *Concepción*.

Young boys' names often end in -*ito* as in Manolito and Panchito; girls' names end in -*ita* (Juanita, Lupita). This is comparable to -*y* and -*ie* in English: Tommy, Johnny, Bobby; Debbie, Christie, Cathy. Just as in English, women are more likely than men to use these diminutive forms well into their adult years.

Like other Hispanics, Mexicans also use descriptive nicknames that might surprise Anglos. *Gordo* (Chubby), *Flaco* (Skinny), *Flaquita* (Skinny Girl), *Pecosa* (Freckles), *Chato* (Pug-Nose),and *Güera* (Blondie) are common nicknames used affectionately with absolutely no connotation of offense. In fact, *Gordita* (Chubby Girl) may be a term of endearment, like Honey in English, even when the girl is quite slender. By contrast, American nicknames referring to physical characteristics (e.g. Fatso, Toothpick, Shorty, and Four Eyes) are most often intentionally cruel.

Spanish Language in the United States

One does not have to go south of the border to find the Spanish

---

[2] All of the present states of Texas, New Mexico, and Arizona, as well as parts of California, Nevada, Utah, Colorado, Oklahoma, and Kansas, were part of the Spanish colonial empire until 1821, when they became part of the newly independent Mexico. The declaration of independence of Texas from Mexico in 1835 led to the Mexican-American War, which resulted in the annexation by the United States of more than half of Mexico's territory in 1848. Even now, many Mexicans bear a tinge of resentment toward the United States for what Mexican history books aptly call "The War of the American Invasion."

Following that war, many Spanish-speaking families remained in the annexed territories, now part of the United States. The descendants of some of these families can trace their roots in the area as far back as the sixteenth century. It is no wonder that the American Southwest has a strong Hispanic flavor.

language. Mexicans living in the United States will encounter many familiar words and place names that have been adapted directly from Spanish. Many of these are common nouns that describe geographic features (canyon, mesquite, mesa) and elements of culture (rodeo, adobe, fiesta) found in the American Southwest.[2] Other familiar words include names of Mexican foods popular throughout the United States, such as taco, enchilada, tortilla, and tamale.

Many place names throughout the American Southwest reflect the devout Catholicism of the early Spanish explorers and colonizers: Santa Fe (Holy Faith), Los Angeles (The Angels), San Diego (Saint James), and San Luis Obispo (Saint Louis the Bishop), to name a few. Other United States place names derived from Spanish describe geographic features: Sierra Nevada (snowy mountain range), Mesa Verde (green tableland), Arizona (arid zone), Florida (flowery), and Montana (mountain). Spanish place names that describe the color of the soil or terrain include Colorado (red-colored), Amarillo (yellow), and Piedras Negras (black stones).

Anglicisms in Mexico

Language, as well as culture, flows across the Mexican-American border in both directions. Due to the proximity of Mexico to the United States, Mexicans use more English words in daily conversation than do Hispanics in most other Spanish-speaking countries. The vocabulary of American sports, especially baseball, has been adopted almost verbatim. The sports section of any Mexican newspaper contains words such as *jonrón* (home run), *jit* (hit), *pléiof* (play-off), *pitcher*, *nócaut* (knockout), *básquetbol*, and *vólibol,* with spelling changes to reflect Spanish pronunciation.

To describe various products of twentieth-century technology, Mexicans have adopted English words such as *walkman, cassette, floppy* (as in 'floppy disk'), *compac* (compact disc) and *elepé* (the Spanish pronunciation of the letters LP, to refer to a long-playing record). In computer classes, Mexican students learn all terminology in English, although they adapt this to Spanish pronunciation. In the next few years, as people from Mexico and the United States have ever more contact with each other, the flow of new words across the border will almost certainly continue.

part of Mexico City, to view from a discreet distance the image of the Virgin imprinted on Juan Diego's blanket and to worship with Catholics from around the world. Due to earthquake damage and other structural problems, the sixteenth-century basilica was condemned in the mid-1970s. The new basilica, modern in architectural style, can accommodate several thousand worshippers at once. Pilgrims may also worship at a small shrine on the very hillside where Juan Diego first saw the vision.

Some Mexicans complain that the vast new basilica fails to inspire the awe of the older baroque-style church; yet the Virgin remains as popular as ever in the Mexican imagination. Today, more than four and a half centuries after her original appearance, the Virgin of Guadalupe has been elevated practically to the level of national symbol and patroness of Mexico.

Rich and poor alike venerate the Virgin of Guadalupe. One can see her image in small shrines in humble homes in the most remote villages. Her image can also be found in virtually every cathedral and church in Mexico, as well as in parochial schools, businesses, markets, buses, taxis, and many homes. In fact, more Mexicans say they believe in the Virgin of Guadalupe than in Christ or even God. December 12, the day of the Virgin of Guadalupe, is an official national holiday, observed with pilgrimages, processions, special masses, fiestas, and Indian dances in front of some churches. In a sense, the Virgin of Guadalupe represents the essence of Mexico, the fusion of two cultures, Catholic Spain and indigenous Mexico.

The Special Role of Saints

In addition to this beloved Virgin, many Mexicans venerate numerous Catholic saints. In colonial times, the panoply of saints facilitated the conversion of Indians to the new faith. Indians were willing to give up their traditional deities once they saw that the new faith, in addition to one great God, had saints who could serve as intercessors, facilitating the arrival of prayers to God. Through the years, the role of saints for Catholics in Mexico has been considerably greater than for Catholics in most other countries.

The Catholic Church is careful to use the word *venerate* when speaking of saints, as opposed to *worship* or *adore,* since Christianity allows the worship of only one God. Yet for many Mexicans, especially for those with little education or sophistication, this distinction may be a fine one.

In fact, the Church was clever in correlating divine functions; many of the saints have conveniently assumed characteristics of certain deities of the Aztecs and other indigenous cultures. Various saints are reputed to be interested in specific areas of concern—health, fair weather, safe   travel, formerly associated with pre-Columbian deities. San Isidro, for example, is the patron of the harvest. Believers turn to San Sebastian with prayers for rain in time of drought. Saint Anthony is the preferred intercessor for prayers from young women seeking husbands.

Today there are chapels dedicated to various saints in most Catholic churches in Mexico. Believers typically light candles to a favorite saint, asking that saint to hasten the arrival of specific prayers or petitions to Almighty God. The statues of the saints are usually hand-painted and nearly always receive exquisite care. Devout parishioners, mostly older single women, volunteer to dress the saints in new clothes every year on their feast day.

A few years ago, the inhabitants of San Cristobal las Casas in the southern state of Chiapas experienced a crisis when the Church announced the official decanonization of Saint Christopher, the saint after whom the town was named. How could the city's beloved patron be stripped of his sainthood? The townspeople maintained that Saint Christopher had protected and assisted them in times of crisis. What right did faraway Vatican officials have to declare otherwise? Despite exhortations from the Church hierarchy and some efforts by Protestant missionaries, the people of San Cristobal have continued to venerate their beloved Saint Christopher.

Catholic Sacraments for Everyone

Of course not all Mexicans subscribe to Catholic dogma. Particularly in the larger cities and among the younger generation, there are many *católicos no-practicantes*, or nonpracticing Catholics, people who were baptized Catholic but who do not attend mass regularly or accept all the doctrines of the Church. Yet even those who scarcely ever enter a church tend to observe certain sacraments within the Catholic faith. These sacraments may include baptism, first communion, confirmation, marriage, and burial. Culturally, if not theologically, even nonpracticing Catholics still feel an affiliation with the Church.

With minor variations, the observance of the sacraments in Mexico is practically the same as in other Catholic countries around the world. Most couples, even nonpracticing Catholics, choose to marry within the church, perhaps "for the sake of the family," but mostly because this is simply the social norm. The wedding ceremony includes a full Catholic mass, during which the couple takes medicine and witchcraft to treat all manner of ailments. Even though the Church preaches strongly against such practices, the *curanderos* remain popular. In fact, *curanderos* from throughout Mexico gather for several days each year in Catemaco, Veracruz, to share their secret wisdom. Their fame as healers may extend far beyond their own village. Some upper- and middle-class Mexicans, even educated urban professionals, secretly seek out the services of a *curandero* in time of crisis.

At the same time, the Catholic priest plays an extremely important role in indigenous villages. Not only does he baptize, confess, marry, and bury members of virtually every family; he also offers spiritual counsel and consolation in time of crisis and is the intercessor for prayers for a good harvest. In most villages, people venerate their priest; in fact, he may be regarded as a higher authority than the law. If a municipal official orders an individual to obey a particular mandate, that person might well go to the priest first to ask whether he should comply.

Separation of Church and State: Anticlericalism

While the power and influence of the priest may be most obvious in small villages, the Catholic Church has been influential in many spheres of activity ever since the days of the conquest. In colonial times and during the early years of independence, the Church held huge tracts of land, essentially controlled education, and provided the only official register of births, marriages, and deaths.

By the mid-nineteenth century, many Mexicans were alarmed by the unchecked power of the Catholic Church. Benito Juárez, the first full-blooded Indian to become president of Mexico, resolved to break the Church's power. In a series of sweeping mandates passed between 1857 and 1861, collectively known as La Reforma (Reform), the church and state were legally separated. Now all Mexicans are required to have a civil registry of birth, marriage, and death. Furthermore, neither the Church nor priests may legally own property; church buildings in Mexico are property of the state. Priests and nuns could not legally vote in national or state elections until the summer of 1992. Religious images have appeared on television only since the Pope's visit to Mexico in 1990.

With few exceptions, Mexicans have adhered to strict observance of separation of church and state since the 1860s. Mexicans do not want anyone from the Church involved in secular events. There are no prayers or invocations to open graduation ceremonies, sports events, sessions of the national congress, or any other public function.

Mexicans do not swear on the Bible in court or anywhere else. Prayer in public schools would be unthinkable and illegal, though prayer is possible in private schools. Presidents and other public officials do not attend mass except privately.

Mexicans are fascinated to learn that the "almighty" American dollar bears the words "In God We Trust." Many Mexicans find this vaguely disturbing; it may appear to them that Americans are confusing God and Mammon.

Despite official separation of church and state, the Catholic Church continues to enjoy considerable influence. The Church maintains close ties with the Mexican government in what sometimes appears to be an interdependent relationship. When Pope John Paul visited Mexico in 1990, government television reported his travels minute by minute. Some observers speculate that the 1992 law allowing priests and nuns to vote is designed to strengthen the church's friendly relationship with the government.

In a country with such an influential church hierarchy, one sometimes hears jokes and irreverent comments about bad priests and corrupt church officials. But one must make a careful distinction between occasional criticism of the Church on the one hand, and devotion to God and the Virgin on the other. Any irreverent comment or joke about Catholic dogma, particularly the Virgin Mary, would be considered highly offensive by almost every Mexican.

Protestants: A Tiny but Growing Minority

While Catholicism is clearly the norm, one does find in every Mexican city a few Protestant churches. These most often represent religious groups with active efforts to proselytize and seek new converts, such as the Mormons, Jehovah's Witnesses, and Seventh-Day Adventists. Other denominations with missionary efforts and churches in Mexico include Baptists and Presbyterians.

The Mexicans who convert to Protestantism tend to be seekers. They may be lonely people seeking friends and affection; they may be disaffected Catholics seeking a religion that better addresses their personal needs.

Most Protestant churches in Mexico give much attention to new members, making every individual feel special and appreciated. Mexicans who have felt lost in their Catholic faith or generally alienated often find a supportive community of believers in a Protestant group.

The Mexicans who do convert for religious reasons tend to be fervent believers, somewhat akin to born-again Christians in the United States. These Protestants must be firm in their convictions, in order to resist the compelling social and cultural norm of the vast Catholic majority.

Other motives for joining a Protestant church may be less laudable. Some "converts" are attracted primarily by the free English lessons, potential contacts leading to travel to the United States, Sunday afternoon basketball games, and other appealing social activities.

Many Mexican Catholics have a limited and somewhat distorted understanding of Protestantism, largely due to overzealous efforts by some missionary groups. Some uneducated Mexicans do not even know that Protestants are also Christians. Those foreign missionaries who come to criticize the particular way that Mexicans worship, pray, and practice their devotion to God and Christ may only offend the sensibilities of a deeply religious people. Besides, there is a deep distrust of some of these groups due to proven contacts to certain United States government agencies. For the foreseeable future, Mexico will remain a Catholic country.

Men and Women

On the Cusp between Tradition and Change

Mexico has long had the reputation as a land of machismo, a sexual double standard, and of traditional male and female roles. In a society where males have always enjoyed privileged status, change does not come easily. Nevertheless, in large part due to the influence of the nearby United States, traditional patterns are starting to give way. Many Mexican women are seeking more opportunities and more nearly equal status; middle- and upper-class men are paying lip service to the concept of equality. Yet despite significant improvement in women's status in the past decade, the respective roles of men and women in Mexico remain vastly different from those in the United States. Deeply rooted patterns of male dominance still permeate all aspects of Mexican culture. In the years ahead, the continuing impulse toward a shift in the traditional paradigm will present challenges for both Mexican men and women.

Historical Reasons for Machismo

The male dominance so characteristic of Mexican culture is deeply rooted in Mexican history. The Spanish conquistadors, fearless adventurers, believed in the natural superiority of man. They came from a warrior society in which men had fought battles against the Moorish infidels for centuries, while women stayed home. During those eight centuries of Moorish occupation of Spain, the Spaniards had absorbed concepts from Islam regarding the inferior status of women. Their cultural heritage also included the tradition of Don Juan, the legendary Spanish nobleman who proved his virility through numerous sexual exploits.

Indigenous cultures also gave favored status to the male. In most pre-Columbian Mexican cultures, men worked in the fields while women tended the home. The woman deferred to the will of the man, who had higher status.

When the bold Spanish conquistadors married the submissive

Indian women, the latter assumed from the beginning that their role would be to serve and obey the men who had conquered their people. The fusion of two male-dominant cultures assured the wide disparity in the status of men and women that has characterized Mexican culture into this century.

The Trials of Being Macho

The word *macho* (literally, male) does not generally carry the negative connotations in Mexico that it often does in the United States. For Mexicans, *macho* implies strength, valor, self-confidence, and masculinity—all positive qualities. An underlying, implicit assumption in Mexican culture is that men are supposed to be stronger, braver, wiser, and more sexually knowledgeable than women. From earliest childhood, Mexican boys are conditioned to appear brave and strong, "like a man." Subconsciously, in myriad ways, Mexican men spend their lives trying to live up to the exaggerated expectations that their culture has demanded of them.

Not permitted to show weakness or fear, Mexican men tend to mask any insecurities they may have behind a facade of bravado and posturing. In the words of James Horn, "The need to prove one's masculinity, often rooted in insecurity, may be manifested in displays of courage (the bull fight), risk taking (behind the wheel of a car), violence (bar room confrontations), and sexual prowess (bragging about one's conquests or siring large families).[1]   Through the years, Mexican women have learned to accommodate this *macho* bravado. With grace and subtlety, they avoid injuring the pride of their husbands, brothers, and sweethearts. Rarely do Mexican women contradict or criticize their husbands in public, though behind the scenes, the woman may often be the power behind the throne.

Chivalry

Most Mexican men are extremely polite and attentive to women, though often somewhat patronizing. The chivalrous attitudes that still flourish in the 1990s are the heritage of earlier times, when men were expected to protect and defend women. All well-bred Mexican men help women across the street, open doors, and make sure to walk

---

[1]James J. Horn, *Cuernavaca: A Guide for Students and Tourists,* 3d ed. (Brockport, N.Y.: Educational Travel Service, 1989), 44.

on the part of the sidewalk next to the street when accompanied by a woman.

Mexican women appreciate these attentions. The fact that women are perfectly capable of opening their own doors is not the point. A woman's refusal of these gestures would be most disconcerting to a man. By accepting these courtesies, women allow men to be gallant and to show proper upbringing.

When a Mexican man invites a woman to dinner, it would be almost unthinkable for him to allow her to help pay the bill. One Mexican who had invited a woman to an elegant dinner realized to his horror at the end of the meal that he had forgotten his wallet. He discreetly excused himself "for a moment" and left his bewildered date sitting alone for more than half an hour while he walked home to get his money. The idea of asking his friend for a loan never occurred to him. Even if he had asked, she would have likely slipped him the money under the table, since traditional Mexican male pride demands that he pick up the check.

As more young women begin to work outside the home, these attitudes are beginning to change, especially in larger cities. Among professional circles, when two young adults go out together frequently, the man and woman are likely to share the bill. The key word in knowing who will pay is *invitar* (to invite). If a Mexican says, "I would like to invite you to my favorite café," this means, "I will pay."

Traditional Gender Roles

The typical Mexican husband aspires to protect and provide for his family, as well as to be strong and *macho*. In a traditional marriage the husband works outside the home while his wife attends to the house and children. The average Mexican husband is five to ten years older than his wife, which gives him the authority of experience. Most Mexican men seek a wife who will be willing to defer to her husband.

For most women the role of mother is primary, even before that of wife. In fact, nearly all Mexicans glorify motherhood. The mother is adored, put on a pedestal like the Virgin Mary; this glorification is called *Marianismo* or, in popular culture, *mamaísmo*. Typically, a Mexican man reveres his own mother and will do almost anything to defend her honor. In a culture where motherhood is practically sacred, the worst insult to a man is for someone to question his mother's honor.

Most Mexican men love to see their wives in the role of mother. Traditionally, men considered a large family as indisputable proof of the husband's virility. Childless couples in Mexico have always been

regarded as odd and even the object of pity.

The Mexican mother reigns as queen of the house. She assumes the primary responsibility of child rearing, especially when the children are very young. The mother is more likely to handle the discipline of younger children. As they grow older, the children tend to fear the father more; he has the final word. The mother, however, does enjoy the children's respect and love. One subtle way that mothers resist absolute domination by the father is to ally with the children to win their loyalty and affection.

The Persistent Double Standard

The double standard regarding sexual mores persists both before and after marriage. When the children reach the older teenage years, sons have much more freedom than daughters. A highlight of a Mexican girl's teenage years is usually her fifteenth birthday, or *quinceaños*. On this occasion, she is the sparkling debutante. After this presentation into society, she is courted, flattered, and even serenaded. At the same time, she is apt to be zealously protected, since her virginity is to be guarded like a precious treasure.

At the marriage altar, the groom is expected to be "experienced," while the bride is supposed to be a virgin, though the ideal of the virgin bride is rapidly losing ground in the cities. To make possible this disparity at the altar, it is common for men to gain experience in houses of prostitution. Most Mexican men still believe there are two kinds of women: the "nice" women who would make good wives and mothers, and sexual playmates. (American women in Mexico should be advised that the Mexicans' stereotype usually places them in the latter category.)

After marriage, the traditional Mexican husband can get away with numerous extramarital affairs. It is still common for a Mexican husband to maintain a second home, the *casa chica* (little house), with a permanent mistress. However, if a married woman is discovered in even one dalliance, her furious husband will most likely file for divorce. Even Mexican men with numerous lovers are apt to list fidelity as the first quality of an ideal wife.

Factors for Change

For a number of reasons, traditional patterns of male dominance are starting to erode. One factor for change has been the nascent women's movement in Mexico. Strongly influenced by the women's movement in the United States, this movement has provided positive role models for Mexican women seeking an identity beyond that of wife and mother, especially in the cities, where there are chapters of women's cooperatives.

Much more far-reaching in its impact is television. In small villages, women see images of products, places, and lifestyles previously undreamed of. While the luxurious lifestyles portrayed on imported American programs may seem remote, Mexican women seem to draw inspiration from strong female characters. A Mayan woman in a village in Yucatán said that the American television series "Dallas" had opened her eyes to the variety of professional options available to women. While retaining her traditional role of wife and mother, she opened a successful business.[2]

Yet another factor for change is the availability of contraceptives; this has liberated women from constant pregnancy. Perhaps surprisingly in this Catholic country, the government distributes contraceptives at no cost in clinics throughout Mexico and sponsors educational programs concerning their use. Acceptance of contraceptives has been gradual but is now widespread. Abortion is against the law and is still very much a taboo subject, though illegal abortions in Mexico are common.

Fewer children per family means a higher standard of living as well as more options for women. The notion that a large family is the best proof of male virility is gradually disappearing.

The degree to which male and female roles in Mexico are changing varies tremendously according to region and socioeconomic class. In isolated villages and rural areas without electricity, men continue to work in the fields, while women tend to the house and children. Both may live out their lives without ever questioning their traditional roles.

On the other extreme of the cultural spectrum, educated women in the larger cities emulate the independent lifestyle of professional women in the United States. Most urban professional men acknowledge the right of women to pursue advanced education and careers, though patronizing attitudes and job discrimination still prevail.

In between these two extremes lie the majority of Mexican men and women, products of Mexico's Catholic mestizo culture. In medium-sized cities throughout Mexico, middle-class Catholic women are beginning to seek broader educational and professional opportunities and more freedom in their social relations.

---

[2]Paula R. Heusinkveld, "Muna Yucatán: A Mayan Village Enters the Mainstream" (Unpublished paper originally presented at the South Eastern Council of Latin American Studies, Mérida, Yucatán, April 4, 1988; revised March 1990), 6.

Women's Liberation—Up to a Point

These kinds of changes, however, will not come easily. For most Mexican men, the notion of "liberation" of the woman is mysterious and threatening. Many assume that the women's talk of liberation is some kind of phase that will eventually pass. Even those Mexican men who claim to be in favor of the liberation of women persist in the traditional assumption of male superiority.

For women, too, change may be threatening. Because women's very identity is embodied in the roles of wife and mother, one cannot automatically assume that liberated is always better. Middle-class Mexican women find themselves on the cusp between the traditional past and a future fraught with uncertainty as well as opportunity. They seek to improve their status without abrogating their role as wife and especially that of mother, which is so essential to their identity.

On a subconscious level, many Mexicans—especially women—still tend to reinforce the old system. Mothers speak of liberation and encourage their daughters to go to the university and "develop themselves." Ironically, many of these same mothers raise their sons to be totally dependent on women to meet their domestic needs. Most upper- and middle-class Mexican men remain helpless in the kitchen, although this is also beginning to change.

Even those mothers who send their daughters off to college admonish them to keep an eye out for marriage as they pursue their education. Mexicans jokingly say that the most popular college degree for women is the M.M.C., or *Mientras Me Caso* (until I get married). For women, marriage is definitely still considered the most desirable option.

Educational Opportunities

Higher education for women in Mexico is gradually becoming more accepted. Many careers, particularly engineering, are still almost exclusively pursued by males. Nevertheless, women are branching out beyond traditional female courses of study such as nursing and teaching to study a variety of other careers including medicine and law. Pharmacy, traditionally a male-dominated field in the United States, attracts many more women than men in Mexico.

In rural areas and small towns, higher education for women is still regarded as a luxury. In many areas, even high school education for girls has been considered unnecessary. Many girls from lower-class families drop out of school to help with the housework, sometimes as early as at the primary school level.

Until 1992, Mexican children were legally required to attend school through only the sixth grade. In May 1992, President Salinas de Gortari announced a sweeping educational reform. The School Reform Act of 1992 makes secondary school (junior high) obligatory for all Mexican children, combining primary and secondary studies as *educación básica* (basic education). This law also shifts control of education from the federal government to the states. With a curriculum tailored to the particular needs and interests of each region, both male and female students are expected to stay in school longer.

The Working World

Following the example of American women, many educated Mexican women seek work outside the home. But in a culture where work is often viewed as a necessary evil rather than a fulfilling activity, many husbands have difficulty understanding why their wives would want to be "liberated." Indeed, some upper-class women accustomed to a life of tennis, bridge, and servants find that full-time employment may be a highly overrated activity. Many prefer the old system, although increasing social pressure to be productive outside the home is beginning to erode traditional patterns of leisurely living.

Still, there are more working women in Mexico every day, though not nearly as many as in the United States. Those women who do work nearly always have less prestigious positions and earn less money than men. In most cases, women work out of economic necessity; the concept of fulfillment through career is widely accepted in Mexico City and other larger cities but is only beginning to take hold in the provinces. In small cities, women who work may be viewed with suspicion: perhaps they are looking for an affair.

One of the greatest sources of frustration for those women who seek liberation from their traditional role is the men's reluctance to help in the house. Even those husbands who agree that their wife should be "allowed" to work outside the house do so on the condition that she can still handle all the responsibilities of housework and child care.

In 1980 six prominent professional men and six equally prominent women from Mexico City were interviewed for a national magazine concerning their views of women's roles.[3] Though all six

---

[3]Interview in *Claudia,* January, 1980.

men said they strongly supported the women's movement, all six confessed that they would not go so far as to help with housework. More than a decade later, these attitudes still prevail, though this is beginning to change among young, urban middle-class couples.

Most Mexican men are loath to help because they feel that housework somehow diminishes their masculinity. The idea that this work is strictly for women persists; in fact, men who do help their wives in the house may be regarded as henpecked fools. Mexican men find the American comic strip "Blondie" appalling. Here the reader laughs as Blondie chases Dagwood around the house to trap him to wash windows or do other housework. This strip, widely circulated in Mexico, has helped to form a stereotype that women in the United States browbeat their emasculated husbands.

Modern conveniences have not freed Mexican women from the kitchen nearly as much as in the United States. Because home-prepared meals remain a high priority, Mexican women do not often choose to take short cuts. While microwave ovens are rapidly becoming more common in middle- and upper-class homes, frozen dinners have not caught on. Since Mexican husbands have a strong cultural bias against working in the kitchen, the women's only path out may be through servants. An upper middle-class woman who takes a job outside the home would be much more likely to contract a maid to help cook and clean than to serve prepackaged meals.

In small villages, one modern convenience, the automatic torti-lla-making machine, has had tremendous impact in freeing women from hours of work each day. In the Mayan village of Muna, Yucatán, one woman reported that she used to spend up to seven hours per day preparing tortillas for her family of five. Now she takes corn to the *tortillería*, where it is ground into corn meal and then made into tortillas automatically in less than an hour. The newfound free time may be spent in making fine embroidered handicraft to sell to tourists or in growing produce for sale in the market. Just as likely, women may spend their time watching television, especially the *telenovelas* (soap operas).

Tradition, Change, and Accommodation

Despite the changing expectations and the apparently modern mind-set of many Mexican women today, they are still traditional in many ways. Most would rather be married than not, and to a large extent they define themselves in terms of their relationships with men. Many Mexican women leave their profession upon marrying. Those who are already married maintain their housewifely duties even as they pursue professions or extend their social circles.

Many vestiges of the old system remain. For example, there are bars for men only. Mexican men defend their right to go to these cantinas. It is here, they say, that they can genuinely relax. With no women present, they can drop the posturing and relax with their male friends. (While women are legally permitted to enter, a strong social taboo generally keeps women from venturing inside a cantina. Bars where women are socially acceptable are called ladies' bars or cafés.)

In one small town in 1991, men crowded into a popular cantina to watch the national soccer finals on the only satellite dish television in the city. Women who happened to be soccer enthusiasts were out of luck, since the men-only rule was strictly enforced.

Mexican women would never consider storming the bar, since this would create more of an uproar than it was worth. In fact, women respect the men's right to their own space, just as men respect women's own space. In Mexico, where machismo is still firmly rooted and femininity is prized, women sense intuitively that direct confrontation with men would be counterproductive.

The shrill rhetoric that has characterized some elements of the women's movement in the United States is entirely absent in Mexico. Unwilling to live in the past, yet not interested in confrontation, Mexican women find subtle, ingenious ways to advance their interests. These include feminine charm, flattery, discretion, guile, and especially accommodation. Without directly challenging their authoritarian husbands, Mexican women achieve a delicate balance between compliance with social norms and the search for self-actualization.

Accommodation does not mean surrender; rather, it is a means to power. On the surface, much remains the same; Mexican women continue to fulfill admirably the traditional roles of wife and mother. Nevertheless, behind the decorous facade of propriety, some Mexican women may have additional agendas. Because discretion is so complete, it is almost impossible to know exactly to what degree Mexican women of the 1990s are stepping out of traditional norms.

A degree of subtlety is required as some Mexican women secretly rebel against the double standard embedded in their culture. Victoria, a prosperous, middle-aged professional woman, told an American sociologist that she knew for a fact that some women her age had extramarital affairs, but that utter discretion is required. She might seek a lover in another city, in a completely different social circle, so that her husband could not find out. For example, she might tell her husband she needed to go to another city—say, Guadalajara—to care for a sick relative.

Victoria insisted that this did not apply to her since she had a good marriage and would not consider infidelity. A week later when the sociologist phoned Victoria's office, she was told Victoria had suddenly been called out of town, to Guadalajara, to visit a sick aunt.

Working and Living

Seeking a Balance

Do we live to work, or work to live? Manuel Rojas, a Mexican doctoral candidate at an American university, was amazed by the behavior of his major professor, a biochemist of national stature. This busy man "saved time" during the lunch hour by snacking on food from vending machines in his office. At best, the professor sent out for a hamburger and french fries, but he virtually never went home for lunch.

Manuel expressed his disbelief to a friend: "Is this your idea of success? This brilliant man holds a prestigious position and earns a handsome salary. Yet he can't even leave his office to enjoy a meal with his family! If work leaves no time to live one's life, then what's the point?"

The professor, of course, is not unique in his behavior. Many Americans stay overtime at the office, miss a family dinner, or even lose sleep to "get the job done right." And despite admonitions to "take time to smell the roses," statistics indicate that many Americans continue to endanger their health for the sake of work. Americans suffer from high rates of heart attacks, high blood pressure, ulcers, and other stress-related disorders.

From the Mexican perspective, these behaviors suggest a severe distortion of priorities. If work consumes all of one's energy and allows little or no time to enjoy the fruits of one's labor, then what is the purpose? Mexicans consider work not as an end in itself, but rather as a means of gaining the economic power to enjoy life with one's family and friends. In fact, a well-known Mexican proverb says that the Anglo-American lives to work, while the Mexican works to live.

Work as a Measure of One's Identity

Our priorities are reflected in the way we introduce people to our friends. At a cocktail party in the United States, one hears, "Meet John Martin. He works with IBM." Or, "Meet Jane Benson. She teaches chemistry at the university." It seems that for Anglo-Americans, one's very identity tends to derive from one's work.

This scenario is less likely in Mexico. More often, people are identified through family relations, their place of origin, or other personal qualities. We might hear, "Meet Magdalena Lozano; she's the cousin of Teresa Lozano de Robles." "Meet Alberto García. He's from Veracruz." Or simply, "This is my friend Mercedes; she's a wonderful person."

One of the first questions that an Anglo-American might ask a new acquaintance is "Where do you work?" This question suggests that a person's paid job is the most essential aspect of one's identity. It also subtly implies that everyone ought to be working for pay.

Mexicans, by contrast, ask a new acquaintance, <<¿A qué te dedicas?>> (literally, "To what do you dedicate yourself?"). This question is more open-ended and less judgmental than the American equivalent. A married woman who dedicates her time to her house and children can answer this question with pride in her domestic accomplishments. A Mexican with a perfunctory job who spends his free time studying the guitar can focus the conversation immediately on what interests him most—his music. On the other hand, a professional who is proud of his career can answer this question by discussing his work. At no moment is there any insinuation that working for pay is better than doing something else, or that one's identity must depend on having a job.

When one's sense of personal identity and self-worth is closely linked with one's work, retirement can be a difficult time. In the United States, some psychologists treat aging clients who suffer trauma after retirement because they feel they have lost a significant part of their identity. This may also occur in Mexico, especially in families where all the children have left home, but to a much lesser degree than in the United States.

The words we choose to talk about retirement in English and Spanish reflect different attitudes toward work. In English, the word *retire* has slightly negative connotations. After a long day, we retire for the night, that is, become inactive; a baseball team is retired after three outs; a shy, timid person has a retiring personality; and at the age of sixty-five, Americans retire, usually losing status and income.

The Spanish word *jubilación* has a totally different connotation. Upon reaching the age of sixty-five, the Hispanic is "jubilated," or "jubilates himself," that is, has a jubilee! This is indeed a time for rejoicing and celebration; one has reached the golden age when one can relax and enjoy life.

Manual Labor

Some Mexican attitudes toward work have deep roots in history. For example, the distaste that many members of the Mexican professional class have for manual labor can be traced all the way back to medieval Spain. For eight centuries, Spaniards fought a holy war to expel from their country the Moors, who had invaded the Iberian peninsula from North Africa in AD 711. Throughout this period of *reconquista* (reconquest) most commerce and manual labor were the business of the "infidel" Moors and Jews. For Spaniards at that time, there were only three respectable occupations: warrior, poet, and priest.

When the Jews and the Moors were expelled from Spain in 1492 and 1502 respectively, the professional and commercial classes disappeared as well. But Spaniards did not turn their attention to commerce at home. In one of the great ironies of history, Columbus discovered America and opened a new world of possibilities for the Spaniards just as the centuries-old *reconquista* was ending.

The religious and nationalistic fervor of the *reconquista* was redirected to the Americas, where Spaniards went to be conquerors, warriors, poets, and priests. These bold conquistadors never supposed for one minute that they had sailed to the New World to do manual labor. By obliging thousands of Indians to provide the work force, the Spaniards could devote themselves to other more "noble" pursuits.

The situation in colonial Mexico was entirely different from that of colonial New England, where the Puritan work ethic was the order of the day. The Puritan colonists were convinced that all must work hard together for the formation of a new society. Hard work, they believed, was a worthy end in itself. "Work is good for the soul!" they told their children. "Work strengthens your character!"

Hispanic conquistadors never accepted the Puritan work concept. In fact, the idea persists today throughout much of Latin America that for an educated, professional person, hard physical labor may be beneath one's dignity. Modern Mexicans, of course, recognize the many abuses perpetuated by Spanish conquistadors of the colonial period. Now, almost five hundred years later, Mexicans engage in virtually every profession.

But a distaste for manual labor and heavy physical work still lingers in the professional and managerial classes. The notion of "fix it yourself" makes no sense at all to a Mexican professional who can afford to hire someone else to do home repairs, yard work, or cleaning. After a long hot day at the office, it's more appealing to enjoy a cool drink than to mow the lawn!

Both Mexicans and Anglo-Americans continue to pass on to their children their respective attitudes toward manual labor. Mexican middle- and upper-class families assume that the parents, particularly the father, should be able to provide for the entire family. In "nice" Mexican families, therefore, the summer provides older children with opportunities for socializing, relaxing, and perhaps taking special courses such as in foreign languages or computers.

If a Mexican son or daughter did accept summer employment, it would probably be a "respectable" office job, perhaps as the assistant to a professional. Only in cases of absolute economic necessity would Mexican parents allow their child to accept a low status job such as construction worker. For this reason, upper- and middle-class host families in Mexico often express amazement when bright young Americans arriving for summer study programs report that they earned money for their trip by selling newspapers, waiting tables, or working construction.

In the United States, by contrast, the Puritan work ethic lives on. Even in the "best" families, parents encourage their teenage children to get part-time jobs, because "a little hard work never hurt anybody." And with the high cost of college education in the United States, summer jobs for young people are almost a necessity.

Horatio Alger: Can Anyone Really Make It?

The Puritan work ethic is only part of the motivation that drives Anglo-Americans to work so hard. More compelling, perhaps, is the conviction that work pays off. Most Anglo-Americans are convinced of the direct relationship between work and success. After all, the United States was settled and founded on the premise that every individual has an equal opportunity, and that work is the key to success. In the nineteenth century, as pioneers forged their way across the American continent, experience seemed to bear out the conviction that the individual has control of his own destiny. Until now, despite socioeconomic and racial inequities in the United States, the idea persists that anyone can make it. Ever popular are the stories of Horatio Alger, the hero of mythical proportion who worked his way up from the bottom.

In Mexico, by contrast, historical experience has not demonstrated that hard work is any guarantee of success. Through most of its history, Mexico has been anything but a land of equal opportunity. In pre-Columbian times, Aztec society was rigidly stratified, with a noble class at the pinnacle and workers far below. Stoic acceptance of one's social class was an important virtue. Any effort to rise above the class into which one was born was considered wrong, an affront to the will of the gods.

The class structure imposed during the Spanish colonial period was just as rigid, with Spanish-born males (*peninsulares*) at the top of the socioeconomic scale, American-born descendants of Spaniards (*criollos*) just beneath, and masses of Indians at the bottom. Even after Mexico gained independence from Spain in 1821, Mexican society continued to be rigidly stratified.

The great Mexican Revolution which began in 1910 corrected many inequities and guaranteed many rights, at least on paper. Thanks to increased socioeconomic mobility in this century, a Mexican born into poverty has a greater chance than ever before to improve his status through hard work.

Yet even now, in the last decade of the twentieth century, working one's way up remains considerably more difficult than in the United States. While successful Anglo-Americans may claim to have fought against impossible odds to get to the top, the socioeconomic barriers that confront Mexicans remain more overwhelming. Thus most Mexicans are still convinced that material success is associated with socioeconomic privilege, good political relations on the job, good luck, and even favoritism more than with hard work.

Perhaps for this reason, there is no Horatio Alger myth in Mexico. By contrast, the kind of story apt to capture the popular Mexican imagination portrays a poor but good-hearted hero who wins the lottery, inherits a windfall, or learns that his sweetheart is a wealthy heiress. In all these tales, the real protagonist is good fortune, or destiny. Even in fiction, Mexicans need a lucky break to rise to the top. In the United States one often hears that people make things happen. The Mexican is more likely to say that things happen to people. This reflects the basic fatalism inherent in the Mexican character.

Orientation toward the Present

Unconvinced that individuals have the power to shape their own destiny, Mexicans tend to focus on the present, the only thing that is certain. This is markedly different from Anglos, who always seem to be looking ahead and planning for the future.

The Mexicans' lack of confidence in their ability to control their future affects behaviors in many spheres. They are infinitely less likely than Anglos to open savings accounts, buy life insurance, or engage in financial planning. The idea of a ten-year plan for one's life seems almost sacrilegious, since only God knows what might happen.

The popular song "Qué será, será" (Whatever will be, will be) expresses well the fatalistic attitude of many Mexicans today. This fatalism is especially prevalent among the lower classes, where people have less confidence in their ability to control events. What foreign observers tend to interpret as passive resignation in some indigenous communities in Mexico is more apt to be a stoic acceptance of a harsh reality, a posture that dates back to pre-Columbian experience.

As socioeconomic barriers continue to fall away and as Mexicans continue to gain confidence in their ability to work toward the future, many seem to draw inspiration from the prayer of Saint Francis of Assisi: "Lord grant me the courage to change the things I can, the serenity to accept the things I cannot, and the wisdom to know the difference."

In the meantime, most Mexicans instinctively follow the Latin admonition *carpe diem* (seize the day). "Let us savor the moment and enjoy today, for tomorrow we die. If we cannot predict or control the future, let us take the time to live every moment as fully as possible."

Business as Usual

Working in and around the System

In the United States, it is often asserted that "it's not *what* you know, but *whom* you know" or "contacts are everything." These statements carry a slightly cynical ring in a country presumed to be the land of equal opportunity. Americans like to think that an individual advances through hard work, not through pull or contacts. If a United States businessman uses personal contacts to get a job or promotion or to get around the system, he is discreet because this smacks of favoritism and using the good old boy network.

Mexicans are more open regarding their use of personal contacts. Because many Mexicans consider the system as unresponsive to the needs of the people, personal contacts are considered practically the only way to do business.

Public Mistrust: Us versus Them

Throughout much of their history, Mexicans have had good reason to mistrust their government and other institutions. The colonial government imposed by the Spaniards in the sixteenth century did not favor the common man; nor did it guarantee personal liberties.

After Mexico gained independence from Spain in 1821, the *criollos* (direct descendants of Spaniards) replaced the Spanish-born as the elite. The new government favored this landed elite, and the Indian majority had no rights at all. The system was not intended to be a government "of the people, by the people, and for the people."

The great Mexican Revolution of 1910 resulted in a new constitution that guaranteed many personal rights—at least on paper. This constitution is still in place. Even so, many of these rights have proven easier to state in writing than to put into practice. Until now, most Mexicans refuse to believe they can count on the government or the system to be on their side. Despite perennial efforts by the government to generate public confidence, there still exists a public mistrust, a feeling of us versus them.

To further complicate matters, Mexican bureaucracy is notoriously cumbersome and inefficient. Mexicans love high-sounding rules and lofty statements of purpose—on paper. Through the years, well-intentioned efforts to create rules have probably only exacerbated the situation. With innumerable regulations and procedures to follow to accomplish anything, Mexicans continue to widen the gap between the correct legal way and the expedient practical way. Going through channels can result in a frustrating series of closed doors and instructions to "come back tomorrow."

Doing Business in Mexico: Contacts Are Everything

Personal contacts have become essential to doing business in Mexico. Almost invariably, Mexicans prefer to seek the help of a friend or relative rather than confront head-on the cumbersome, unfriendly bureaucracy.

In order to do business with a new associate, one must first establish a relationship based on personal trust. A Mexican wants to know with whom he is dealing before considering any transaction. Thus, when two businessmen meet for the first time, their meeting usually follows a leisurely pace, with amenities of coffee or drinks. Conversation often turns to their families, since Mexicans consider the family an essential part of one's identity. Whereas an Anglo-American might think, "I don't know this man well enough to ask about something as personal as his family," most Mexicans would think, "How can I possibly get to know this person without knowing about his family?" Business cards are absolutely essential as a courtesy and as a way of maintaining contacts.

In subsequent meetings, both parties continue to cultivate this personal working relationship. The friendship is seen not as an expedient means to an end, but rather as a worthy end in itself. What is more important than to have friends and associates whom one can trust?

In some cases, loyalties to people may remain stronger than loyalties to institutions. Once trust and friendship have been established, a Mexican might prefer to do business with the same individual, even if the latter were to switch jobs to another company.

Palanca: Having the Right Connections

The word *palanca* literally refers to a lever or scaffold, the kind that allows a construction worker or painter to rise rapidly up the outside of a building. But *palanca* has come to mean pull or influence. A Mexican who has a *palanca* can take short cuts because he has personal connections with the people in charge. In order to do business, one should either have a *palanca* or know people who do.

What can one's contacts do for a friend? They can move one past the outer office to speak directly with an executive. They can bypass bureaucratic regulations, cut through mountains of paperwork, and speed up things. They can get a contract for a friend, instead of with the competitor.

Job hunters in Mexico know that a personal recommendation is nearly always more important than the most brilliant résumé. In fact, many positions would be difficult if not impossible to obtain without a strong personal recommendation. This is often true in the United States, but much more so in Mexico.

Following the rules to the letter is less important than being loyal to and honest with one's friends. If an individual takes a legal shortcut to get out of a bind, the "friend" who reports him to the authorities may be considered more culpable than the one who committed the original offense because that friend has proven himself disloyal. In fact, the expression *cooperating with the authorities* often has negative connotations in Mexico, implying betrayal.

The Ubiquitous *Mordida*

When a Mexican is caught in a bind with no friend to bail him out, there is always the *mordida* (literally, bite or bribe). The practice of bribing has almost become institutionalized, particularly in the area of traffic fines. If a police officer stops a Mexican for speeding, the two come to an agreement convenient for both. To avoid the inconvenience of having to report to the transit office to pay a fine, the motorist pays the officer a small amount, and the violation is never reported. The low salaries of traffic officers compound the problem; even officers who have honest inclinations feel the need to collect bribes to make ends meet. Even though the government has begun to pay lip service to ending the *mordida* system, change to date is almost not apparent.

Most Mexicans who bribe government officials do not feel they have committed any terrible crime. Since public perception of government misspending is so widespread, being straightforward with the government is not a priority. Most Mexicans view bribes as a necessary part of life. In Mexico, the idea of bribing a traffic official is probably no more or less common than fudging a little on one's income tax deductions in the United States. Everyone knows it's wrong, but people do it as long as they think they can get away with it. The justification is, "I need the money more than the government does." In Mexico, even more than in the United States, one's first priority is to look out for oneself and one's friends and family.

Corporate bribes are also widespread. Establishing a new business often requires tremendous amounts of paperwork that would result in loss of valuable time and potential earnings. A quick *mordida* to an official can smooth the way and move everything along faster. Corporate bribes also help win contracts, bypass environmental regulations, and take shortcuts on building standards. After the disastrous Mexico City earthquake in 1985, cynical Mexicans noted that nearly all of the buildings that sustained the heaviest damage were those built under government contract. It became evident to all that those buildings had not been constructed according to codes.

Some American companies had to close operations in Mexico after a United States congressional ruling made bribes to foreign companies illegal. The American companies simply couldn't keep up with the competition without the option to bribe.[1]

Beating the System

The concept of us versus them is an insidious one. Since Mexicans regard the government and the system it represents almost as an adversary, beating the system at its own game becomes a popular pastime.

Mexicans who are impeccably honest with their friends and family occasionally flout the rules, almost as a diversion. For example, if a well-mannered, middle-class youth manages to jump the turnstile in the subway station without paying, he expects his friends to be pleased and amused. This is not necessarily considered wrong, just an individual expression of beating the system.

The notion of beating the system may affect behavior in many different areas, including education. Actions that Anglos would condemn as cheating are not usually viewed the same way in Mexico. In a school class during final exam week, students feel a strong bond; they all hope that everyone makes it. The students may indeed cooperate (share information), so that all can succeed. The teacher, the authority figure, represents the system. The student who reports an instance of cheating to the teacher is scorned by his peers as the *chismoso* (tattletale). He has shown himself to be disloyal to his friends and interested only in his own advancement at the expense of others. In the mind of most Mexicans, the *chismoso* has committed

---

[1]See Alan Riding's discussion of all aspects of corruption in the chapter "Corruption: Oil and Glue" in *Distant Neighbors*, 113-133.

a crime far greater than the student who copied another's work in the first place.

Thus, in school, as in business, loyalty to friends takes priority over loyalty to the establishment or strict adherence to rules. In a country where mistrust of the system is so deeply ingrained, change is not likely to come easily. Americans who wish to get along with Mexicans would do best to understand that each culture has a different concept of what is the right way to do things.

Dress and Appearance

Always a Sense of Dignity

Mexicans attribute more importance to behaving and dressing with dignity than do most Anglo-Americans. This sense of dignity, which extends across all social classes and all ages, begins with an individual's sense of self-worth and self-respect. Every Mexican, no matter how poor, expects that as a unique individual and a member of the human community, he should be treated with respect and decency.

Social Interaction: Looking Respectable

The Mexicans' finely honed sense of dignity affects many areas of daily life, including social interaction with others, manners, and personal appearance. Mexican adults are not so apt to let down their hair or to engage in silly behavior as are Americans at play. Sometimes in the United States, the boss or upper management of a company might organize a picnic or other casual social event in which the upper management dresses down to mingle with the employees. Baseball, hot dogs, casual dress, and beer send the message, "We're all part of the same team. The boss is just one of the fellows, too."

This scenario is unlikely in Mexico. Upper management and employees would not be likely to mingle socially, but if they did, the Mexican management might plan an elegant reception for which employees would dress up. In Mexico, lower level employees generally make an effort to match the manners, behavior, and dress of their superiors instead of vice versa.

Public officials and other important people in Mexico are not likely to laugh at themselves. They prefer to retain their sense of dignity and respectability at all times. Certain kinds of fund-raising events that might occur in the United States—a dunking machine where students try to dunk the teacher—are almost unthinkable in Mexico. Mexicans in high positions would not intentionally create a situation that might make them look ridiculous.

Perhaps because Mexicans never receive official permission to laugh at their superiors, they enjoy jokes about important people. Always popular are jokes that expose politicians in their fraud, priests in their dalliances, or public officials in their undignified moments. The humor comes from stripping important people of their dignified facades and exposing them as being ordinary people.

Mexicans in lower positions don't want to appear ridiculous either. Therefore, a Mexican employer would never intentionally embarrass or poke fun at an employee, particularly in front of other workers. Good Mexican managers know that in order to keep their employees' cooperation and respect, they should convey any necessary criticism of an employee's performance as gently as possible and in private.

Mexicans do not usually laugh at anyone who might already be the object of pity. There are apparently no jokes in Mexico about handicapped people, retarded people, or oppressed minority groups, such as one may hear in the United States.

The Importance of *Buena Presentación*

The importance of appearing respectable affects Mexican ideas about dress and appearance. Personal appearance is so important in Mexico that employers seeking new recruits routinely advertise in the newspapers for a candidate with *buena presentación* (literally, good presentation). This is actually listed as a job requirement for most positions that involve meeting the public.

Buena presentación begins with an overall nice appearance: clean, neat, well groomed, well manicured. In addition, *buena presentación* implies good manners, polite speech, and smooth social interaction. A candidate with an unkempt appearance or poor social skills has little or no chance of getting hired, no matter how impressive his other qualifications. While this may be generally true in the United States, it is even more important in Mexico.

Dressing for Success, Mexican Style

Whereas Anglo-Americans highly value a healthy, fit, natural look, Mexicans emphasize careful grooming. Dress does not have to be fancy or expensive, but neatness is essential. Well-dressed Mexican women are well coiffed, carefully made-up (especially eye makeup), and always perfectly manicured. Mexican men wear shoes polished to a high gloss. Even the most humble male employee would have an ironed shirt.

In Mexico, elegance in personal appearance usually takes priority over expensive appointments for the home. Whereas a bride in the United States may register patterns for china, crystal, and sterling silver, Mexicans are more likely to invest in expensive jewelry. Even lower middle-class Mexicans, both men and women, enjoy wearing gold. Mexican men and women of the nouveau riche class often wear diamond-studded watches and valuable rings to dazzle and impress.

Compared to Anglo-Americans, Mexicans place somewhat less importance on a trim, slim figure as part of overall appearance. The time that an American woman might spend in aerobic classes, a Mexican woman might dedicate to a manicure and coiffure. In fact, the Mexican male's ideal of feminine beauty is approximately ten to fifteen pounds heavier than the Anglo-American counterpart. Some slender American beauties may appear too skinny, or almost anorexic, by Mexican standards.

Sometimes Casual but Never Sloppy

As in so many areas of life in Mexico, times are changing concerning dress. While Mexicans tend to dress more formally than Anglo-Americans, casual clothing is becoming more popular. Slacks for women are quite acceptable now for many occasions, and jeans are popular for both men and women. Younger teens are beginning to wear informal clothes fashionable north of the border. T-shirts with logos from American universities are the rage among young people. But casual must never be confused with sloppy. An upper-class Mexican woman may wear slacks to a picnic, but her makeup, hair, and manicure will be perfect. If she wears a T-shirt, it will be carefully ironed. If she wears sandals, her toenails probably will be carefully manicured.

Mexicans also have an acute sense of just where they can dress casually and where they should dress up. Sloppy dress in university classes is generally unacceptable. Most female students still wear dresses and high heels to university classes, and most men wear a nice shirt and slacks, though dress is gradually becoming more casual here, too. Bermudas are beginning to appear in some Mexican universities where there are no formal dress codes. What always distinguishes the Mexican from his United States counterpart are impeccably clean shoes, jewelry, and carefully groomed hair. Even the most casually dressed girl wouldn't be seen without what Americans might consider heavy eye makeup and stockings—even if she's wearing shorts!

Short shorts are appropriate for the beach, sports activities, and in smaller cities in the tropics, but generally are not worn downtown in major cities, though this is also changing. When in doubt, most Mexicans would choose to err on the side of overdressing, rather than dressing too casually.

For Mexican women, attractive, feminine appearance usually takes priority over practicality or comfort. At a party, a woman might refuse to put on a sweater if it did not match her dress, even if she were shivering from the cold. When buying shoes, many Mexican women consider only fashion, practically ignoring comfort. No matter how pressed for time, most Mexican women would not even run an errand to the supermarket without lipstick, eye shadow, and carefully coiffed hair. The idea of wearing hair curlers to the store in Mexico would be inconceivable.

In some cases, women's insistence on attractive dress may limit physical activity. At parties, some upper-class Mexican women wear fashionable pants so tight they can't sit down the entire evening. Young women at a picnic would be unlikely to participate in a game such as volleyball, where they might break a carefully manicured fingernail or perspire and ruin their makeup. At the Mayan ruins of Palenque in the state of Chiapas, a Mexican woman was observed trying to climb the highest pyramid in four-inch high heels. Of course, she needed a hand from her man, who gallantly helped her to climb the irregular steps of the temple.

Decent Dress For All Social Classes

In Mexico, as in many other developing countries, some people of lower socioeconomic classes cannot afford fancy clothes, but any Mexican who can afford to dress decently will do so. Even Mexicans of the humblest social class will make sacrifices to buy decent clothes. A Mexican would almost rather go hungry than appear on the street in tattered clothes or rags.

Therefore, the notion of dressing "poor" intentionally seems absurd to Mexicans. Mexicans wear neat, well-fitting jeans, never jeans that are torn at the bottom or showing holes or slashes at the knees. Many Mexicans, especially those of the older generation, are mystified as to why faded jeans often cost more in fashionable boutiques than jeans that look new. The rationale for wearing ragged cutoffs is even more of a mystery.

No Mexican who can afford a pair of shoes would dream of walking barefoot on the street. Even in the house, Mexicans do not go barefoot (perhaps in part because most Mexican homes have cold tile floors). Mexicans would almost never kick off their shoes at other people's houses and would not think of putting their feet on other people's furniture, for example, on a coffee table.

For the sake of decency, Mexicans tend to be somewhat more covered up than Americans. While halter tops for young women are starting to appear in a few more tropical cities, many Mexicans still consider such provocative dress as vulgar. In Mexican fashion magazines, the women designated as worst dressed of the year are apt to be those who show the most cleavage. Mexican men are also more covered up. Even when engaged in heavy physical labor or an active game of tennis, they wear at least a T-shirt. Usually Mexican men go bare chested only at the beach.

Respect for social norms is much more important in Mexico than personal statements made through bizarre dress. The intentionally sloppy look that for some American adolescents may represent personal independence or rebellion makes no sense to most Mexican teenagers. Mexican teens emulate well-dressed adults. For parties, dances, and fancy occasions, they dress to the hilt. Even those few individualistic Mexican teens who want to make a daring personal statement will dress up, not down, choosing styles that are provocative as well as elegant.

For informal occasions such as picnics, Mexican teens often dress casually with jeans and T-shirts, but like their parents, they are always well groomed. In most places, even the most modern young women who might wear faded jeans or even cutoffs would make sure they fit perfectly and were accompanied by a fashionable belt, a carefully ironed T-shirt, jewelry, perfume, and impeccable makeup, hair, and manicure.

Mexican Time and American Time

There's a Place for Both

Every culture in the world views time in its own particular way. The Chinese, for example, see time as an eternal flow from season to season over the centuries. Anglo-Americans pay careful attention to the clock, trying to maximize their efficiency during each hour of every day. Time in Mexico is more open-ended than in the United States, more flexible and more fluid.

Talking about Time

A well-known American proverb warns us that "time waits for no man." In the United States, time is viewed as a precious, scarce commodity. Americans are therefore encouraged to start earlier since "the early bird catches the worm," and to move faster to "beat the clock." No wonder foreign visitors to the United States often comment that everyone seems to be in a hurry, even though another proverb warns us that "haste makes waste." Time management is just as important to Americans as money management, since "time is money."

The Mexican view of time corresponds more closely to an old Irish proverb: "The man who made time made plenty of it." As Mexicans see it, life is to be enjoyed; therefore, life in Mexico tends to move at a more relaxed pace than in the United States. Speakers of Spanish never talk about *being* late. In fact, according to the Spanish language, it is not possible to *be* late; rather, the latecomer simply *arrives* late.

The Spanish words *a tiempo* (on time, in time) most often refer to important things that have nothing to do with the clock, as in, "The doctor arrived in time to save the patient." If a person arrives promptly for a four o'clock meeting, Spanish speakers simply say that he arrived *a la hora* (at the hour).

Punctuality versus Flexibility

Most people in the United States place a high value on arriving at each appointment precisely at the designated hour. Punctuality is equated with responsibility and efficiency, both important values in Anglo-American culture, while late arrival, pejoratively referred to as tardiness, suggests the opposite. Such extreme attentiveness to the clock does not come naturally to a Mexican, who prefers a more relaxed approach to life. For an American in the habit of being punctual, the Mexicans' relatively casual attitude concerning the clock may be maddening at first. But one must understand that the entire concept of time is different.

Depending on the situation, Mexicans can and do arrive at the designated hour, known as *hora americana* (American time). But Mexicans have a very different sense of which situations require exact attention to the clock and which do not. For most occasions, Mexicans live by the more flexible *hora mexicana* (Mexican time).

To understand Mexicans' attitudes about time, the foreigner needs to know: (1) for which events Mexicans consider it important to arrive on time, (2) to which events Mexicans plan on arriving late, (3) how big a window of time for lateness is acceptable for various events, and, most importantly, (4) what other values take priority over punctuality. What is the Mexican doing while the impatient gringo is waiting at the appointed place?

The Mexican philosophy of savoring the moment can and often does make people arrive late to whatever comes next. If one is enjoying the present moment, why rush on to something else? It may not be as interesting. Whatever is happening now may take priority over punctual arrival to an appointment later on. For example, if a Mexican runs into an old friend en route to an appointment, he will at least say hello and chat for a minute or two. A Mexican would almost never say, "Hi. Can't talk now. Bye." Almost invariably, conversation with a friend takes priority over precise arrival time.

People in the United States sometimes speak of the tyranny of the clock; most Mexicans simply do not allow the clock to rule their lives. The clock will not prevent a Mexican from enjoying that second cup of coffee or that extra moment of pleasant conversation with a friend.

Furthermore, there is no need to arrive at an appointment out of breath or panting or sweating. What is the point of having a heart attack rushing to beat the clock? From the Mexican viewpoint, it seems much better to arrive ten or fifteen minutes late, relaxed.

Events that Demand Punctuality

Even though punctuality does not generally receive high priority in Mexican culture, the clock sometimes does matter. For certain events, Mexicans can and do arrive at the time specified.

Most Mexicans, for example, arrive punctually for job interviews and key meetings with important business contacts. In the incident at the beginning of this book, Mr. Ibarra would have arrived punctually at 4:00 if Mr. Lawson had simply said, "Come at 4:00." Lawson's instructions to come "from 4:00 to 5:00" were totally misleading to Mr. Ibarra, since Mexicans would never state an ending time for an appointment. Also, most Mexicans arrive more or less on time (within ten minutes or so) to doctor's appointments, dental appointments, university exams, and professional meetings.

The privilege of being late is sometimes implicitly associated with one's level of importance. A client is expected to arrive on time to a business appointment, but the boss may not emerge from his office immediately. An applicant for a job is expected to be punctual for the interview, but the employer may keep the applicant waiting in the reception room for some time. This is also a likely scenario in a doctor's office, as it is in the United States. Some Mexican doctors even refuse to make appointments.

Buses between cities nearly always depart precisely at the announced time; knowing this, Mexicans do arrive punctually at the station. The time of arrival at the city of destination, however, may vary. For longer bus trips, time for a leisurely lunch en route is often scheduled into the trip. If the bus driver orders another cup of coffee, the bus may leave a little late after lunch. Occasionally a bus driver might even announce an unscheduled breakfast or lunch stop if his stomach is growling. Bus drivers have also been known to stop at a roadside stand if they spot a good bargain. Mexican passengers seem unperturbed by such unexplained delays, or are at least resigned to them.

In small towns, where the pace of life is more leisurely, local second-class buses may wait until the bus fills up before leaving. For some routes, there is no schedule at all, except to leave whenever people are ready. In small towns and villages, many families do not own a clock. Office workers often do not even use a watch. Time flows according to sun time; one lives by the natural rhythms of each day.

In most cities, movies begin punctually at the announced hour. Most public performances such as concerts and theatrical productions begin close to the hour, although this varies widely from city to city. Scheduled sports events such as soccer matches generally begin on time. Bullfights in Mexico City are famous for their punctual beginnings. Catholic masses begin at the scheduled hour, although many worshipers arrive late. Funerals also begin on time.

Some informal lectures and musical programs may begin whenever the audience seems to be ready. A special lecture by a visiting expert was scheduled in a Mexican university at 5:00 on a weekday afternoon. At 4:55, the first people were arriving to find the room locked. At 5:05, the speaker and those accompanying her arrived with the keys to the room. By 5:25 the room was filled and the lecture began, with no apparent concern on the part of lecturer or audience about the hour.

Everything is Open-ended

In the United States, people live in blocks of time, even for social engagements. An American invitation might read, "Open house: 3:00 - 5:00 Sunday." Such an invitation would be almost inconceivable in Mexico, since it severely violates Mexican rules of hospitality, as well as contradicts the Mexican's more flexible concept of time. When Mexicans open the doors to their home, the invitation is open until the guests feel ready to leave. As long as the guests are enjoying themselves, the party flows on.

The same concept carries over into the business world. While most meetings and appointments have designated times for starting, there is usually no specified ending time. Meetings in Mexico move at a more leisurely pace and run their natural course. Mexican businessmen space out their appointments accordingly, with fewer scheduled meetings for each day. In case of an overlap, the meeting already in session would generally take priority over a prompt beginning for a subsequent appointment.

Because American businessmen want to get to the bottom line, they try to proceed as efficiently as possible to bring a meeting to conclusion, in order to get on to the next task. In America, the *result* is what matters. In Mexico, the *process* is more important. The human interaction that takes place during the meeting is more important than in the United States; rushing to the bottom line matters less. In fact, in a Mexican business setting, too much rushing might endanger the desired outcome.

Most Mexicans go through life without an appointment book. The American concept of a "day-timer," which allows its user to plan each day's activities and tasks into precise blocks of time, is still foreign to many Mexicans. Such exact planning would probably be too rigid, since it would not allow for a natural flow of events.

Not surprisingly, most routine business transactions in Mexico tend to take somewhat longer than in the United States. But Mexicans are not likely to display signs of impatience such as glancing constantly at a watch. Whereas an American standing in line in a bank may be acutely aware of the inexorable ticking away of precious minutes and seconds, a Mexican would more likely be chatting with a friend or simply waiting patiently. From the Mexican viewpoint, fidgety Americans in such circumstances may seem rude, abrupt, or even obnoxious. In a culture where politeness is valued more than efficiency, overt displays of impatience are almost always counter-productive. Americans in Mexico who stare at the clock, fidget, or glare at the bank teller will almost certainly receive slower service than those who wait calmly, since Mexicans perceive the former as impolite and undeserving of respect.

At home, in business, and in school, each activity takes as long as it takes; whatever doesn't get finished today can be done tomorrow. For most Mexicans, the idea of using a clock as a tyrannical measure of performance seems absurd.

Fashionably Late

Despite the importance of the clock in the United States, Americans can and do bend the rules about time for selected occasions. They might arrive "fashionably late" to certain social events, especially in the evening. Just when is it fashionable to be late? How late is fashionable?

Due to their more flexible notion of time, Mexicans instinctively and naturally arrive fashionably late to almost everything, but especially to social engagements.

When Mexicans agree to meet at a cafe at 6:00, a 6:15 arrival would generally require no apology or explanation. It is generally assumed that both parties have about a half-hour window of time.

Evening parties generally start very late. In fact, arrival at an evening party at precisely the announced hour would likely prove to be an imposition on the host and hostess; they might still be in the shower.

An American woman who was new in Mexico announced a dinner party for 8:00. When nobody had showed up by 10:00, she was depressed and started getting ready for bed. When all her friends showed up *en masse* between 10:30 and 11:00, they wondered why she was in her robe!

After the same woman had lived in Mexico for many years, she commented that her American recipes didn't work for Mexican dinner parties, since they require a precise amount of baking time and start drying out or burning if left in the oven too long. These recipes work only in a society where guests arrive precisely at the announced time. Most Mexican recipes, on the other hand, improve the longer they are left in the oven, allowing time for guests to arrive fashionably late.

Taking Time to Smell the Roses

In work and in play, life in Mexico tends to move at a more relaxed pace than in the United States. Mexicans do not need to be reminded to "take time to smell the roses"; they do so instinctively.

Mexicans may joke with American visitors about their lack of punctuality and even profess their intentions to pay more attention to the clock. However, more attention to punctuality would mean a shifting of priorities. In Mexico, human interaction remains more important than efficiency.

Despite concessions to American time, particularly in larger cities, most Mexicans continue to adhere to their own approach to time, especially for social events. Visitors should be patient with Mexican time; it helps to keep life more relaxed.

The Art of Manners

Our Do's and Don'ts Are Different

While every culture has prescribed behavior for smooth interaction with others, some cultures place more emphasis on the observance of prescribed norms than others. Also, specific do's and don'ts vary widely from one culture to the next. Mexicans are generally extremely conscious of the importance of good manners. In fact, manners are so important in Hispanic culture in general that the Spanish words for *good manners* and *good education* are identical. In other words, learning polite behavior is fundamental to one's education and upbringing.

However, the words *buena educación* do not imply a series of memorized formulas. For most Mexicans, the essence of good manners is considerate, respectful treatment of others. A Mexican who displayed impeccable table manners and perfect etiquette in society but who treated his employees rudely would not be considered well bred. In fact, some nouveau riche in Mexico often unwittingly reveal their lower-class origins by their poor treatment of servants and others of humble status. Mexicans who are truly well bred are expected to treat people of all classes with dignity and respect under all circumstances.

Taking Time to Be Polite

Mexicans take time to be polite. This politeness occurs in all sorts of situations, ranging from asking directions on the street to making a telephone call. Traditionally, when telephoning someone, a well-bred Mexican might say, "Good afternoon, Señora, how are you? My name is Roberto Morales, and I am trying to reach María. Does she happen to be at home? Could you be so kind as to call her to the phone? Thank you so much."

This elaborate telephone etiquette has been rapidly disappearing since the spring of 1990, when the Mexican telephone company began to bill local calls by the minute. Mexican teenagers, less bound by traditional etiquette, are especially eager to save money with a quick "Is Elena there, please?" While this direct approach is rapidly becoming more common, it still may seem abrupt or even rude to many Mexicans, especially to those of the older generation.

Despite the changes in telephone etiquette, social niceties continue to take precedence over rushing through most transactions. At a store, for example, Mexicans generally take the time to thank the clerk and wish them a good day. <<*Que le vaya bien*>> ("May it go well with you") is a phrase that concludes dozens of business transactions daily. In smaller cities and provincial capitals, taxi drivers often wish passengers a pleasant afternoon as they leave the taxi.

Deferring to Older People

Manners are especially important when interacting with older people. At family gatherings and other intergenerational events, Mexican children learn to feel comfortable around older people to a degree seldom seen in their Anglo-American counterparts. Mexican children learn at an early age to let older people know they are valued and appreciated.

Special attentions may include extending a warm greeting to older people, making sure they are comfortably seated, or taking time to engage them in conversation. The deference and respect that Mexican children show older people are not artificial formulas; they represent genuine respect and affection.

Mexicans are also careful to show respect to anyone with a professional status or title. Professional people are often addressed by their title instead of their name; one hears, for example, "Good morning, Doctor," "Good afternoon, Professor." Even after a professional person retires, when the real power of a business has passed to younger associates, senior officials enjoy deferential treatment by everyone around them.

Tact: The Art of Telling People What They Want to Hear

Sometimes Mexicans are so polite that they tell people what they want to hear, even when it may not be quite true. In other words, tact is generally valued more highly than directness. Thus, if a Mexican woman asks a friend for an opinion on her dress or hairstyle, the friend would try to find something positive to say, even if she didn't care for it. Everyone is so polite that at first it may be difficult for an outsider to read between the lines and to know what is going on.

The Mexicans' tendency to be helpful and polite under all circumstances can become maddening to a newcomer who is asking for directions. Like most other Hispanics, a Mexican is so eager to appear friendly and helpful that he would rather provide directions— even if they are no good—than to admit not knowing where something is! A Mexican might offer helpful directions with a smile, along a route that doesn't actually exist. The newcomer who is lost would be wise to ask directions several times of several different people.

Another common situation that may lead to frustration for a newcomer occurs in dozens of minor business transactions daily. "Your shoes will be repaired by tomorrow," says the Mexican vendor with a smile. This reassuring statement makes the customer happy for the moment and sounds good, but it may not always correspond to reality.

Hellos and Good-byes: A Personal Touch

Greetings and leave-takings are considerably more elaborate in Mexico than in the United States. Well-bred Mexicans always shake hands when greeting someone, and usually shake hands to say good-bye as well. If a woman arrives a little late to a social gathering, she is likely to greet every single woman present individually with an embrace and a light kiss on the cheek. Even if this interrupts a meeting, it's all right. The human interaction is the most important aspect of the meeting.

When two men greet after a long absence or on special occasions, they are apt to embrace each other, along with a series of gentle pats on the back called *palmadas*. When Mexican men are ready to say good-bye, they usually shake hands with everyone present. At the end of a meeting or social gathering, Mexican women traditionally embrace and kiss every woman present once more.

The physical touching that accompanies hellos and good-byes is just one small aspect of body language. Mexicans stand closer together than Anglos when talking to each other and are more apt to touch in the course of the conversation. In fact, many Mexicans find Anglos to be cold or aloof.

Conclusion: How Can an Outsider Fit In?

In sum, everything moves a little more slowly in Mexico, but there is more human interaction. Mexicans are more apt to take the time for social niceties than Anglo-Americans. Tact and consideration of the feelings of others are valued more highly than directness. From the Mexican viewpoint, Mexicans are tactful and considerate; Anglos, by comparison, may seem rude and abrupt.

A foreigner is not expected to be familiar with all the do's and don'ts of Mexican culture. Knowing the exact protocol for each situation is not as crucial as treating others with consideration and respect. Good upbringing, for Mexicans, is not a series of learned behaviors, but rather a frame of mind, a way of interacting with other human beings.

Expressions of appreciation are important in every culture, but especially in Mexico. A smile is universal, and transcends cultural barriers. When in doubt, a sincere thank-you, a warm smile, and general respect and consideration of others are the essentials.

Mi Casa Es Su Casa

(My House Is Your House)

Often, when a Mexican has just barely made a new acquaintance, he is apt to say, "I live in such and such a house, on such and such a street. *Mi casa es su casa.* My house is your house. Do come by whenever you want." This invitation is almost automatic to Mexicans, something similar to the expression in the southern United States, "Y'all come by sometime!"

While the desire to receive a new friend in one's home is generally sincere, most Mexicans do not actually expect that friend to appear at the door at any time whatsoever. Because the role of host or hostess implies more responsibilities and is more formal in Mexico than in Anglo-American society, dropping in unexpectedly might prove to be an imposition. The most appropriate thing to do would be to wait for a specific invitation for a particular day or to invite the other person first.

Mexicans consider hospitality and generosity extremely important values. No matter how much or how little they have, Mexicans do their best to share whatever they have with others.

Attentive Hosts and Thankful Guests

The supreme importance of generosity in Mexican culture affects the respective roles of host/hostess and guest. The Mexican host offers all that he has to his guests; the only responsibility of a well-bred guest is generally to express ample appreciation and compliments. Rather than help with the work or contribute to the financing of a party, a good Mexican guest thanks the host warmly for all attentions received and then makes a point of returning the invitation and entertaining in comparable style in the near future.

Upon arriving at a Mexican home, a guest is apt to hear, *Esta es su casa* ("This is your house"). In other words, "I'm offering you all that I have; all that is mine is yours." This is not an exact equivalent of the American expression, "Make yourself at home." In the United

States, these words may imply privileges to kick off one's shoes, open the refrigerator, mix oneself a drink, and engage in other casual behavior. This is generally not true in Mexico, except in the case of very close friends. A Mexican guest would not normally offer to make himself a drink or serve himself from the refrigerator. The kitchen is generally considered to be the private domain of the hostess. Also, such actions might imply that the host was not being attentive enough to the guests.

The Mexican host feels completely responsible for the well-being of the guests. Almost invariably, the host or hostess offers guests something to eat or drink, even if there is nothing available in the house. This offer is almost a ritual of hospitality. In humble homes, a guest might do well to refuse the first offer for drink or refreshments, realizing that the host might not actually have what is being offered. In a very humble home, a guest who immediately accepts the first offer of drink or refreshment might have to wait while a family member discreetly slips out of the house to run to the store for whatever has been requested.

The system of potluck has never been the norm in Mexico; generally the host or hostess is responsible for the preparation and serving of all food. This convention is changing in some cities, especially in circles of busy professionals. Even so, guests would be more likely to take dessert or drinks than a main dish.

Curiously, when a guest compliments the hostess on the delicious food, the appropriate response would not be "Thank you." That might imply, "Thank you for recognizing my wonderful cooking ability!" A more appropriate response would be, "Oh, is it good? I'm so glad!" or "Anything for you, my friend!"

A good Mexican host or hostess attentively refills drinks, offers second helpings of food, and makes every effort to make sure the guests are comfortable. A well-bred Mexican guest, no matter how thirsty or hungry, waits until the hostess offers to serve rather than asking for something directly. This system may take some getting used to for Anglo-Americans, who are more direct about making their needs known.

Even if food is set out in buffet style, Mexicans wait for a specific invitation to begin eating. At an evening reception, a sumptuous buffet spread may sit untouched for hours, since Mexicans often wait until near the end of the evening to eat. Once the invitation to eat has been extended, most Mexican men still expect the women to fill their (the men's) plates from the buffet. Many Mexican women claim— only half in jest—that their husbands would starve before serving themselves. Mothers also fill the plates of their children. Thus, even when they are guests in another home, Mexican women continue to serve their family.

It is uncommon for Mexican guests to offer to help clean up, except in the case of very close friends. In fact, guests in Mexican homes would not normally enter the kitchen, or anywhere else beyond the public areas of the house (living room, dining room, and possibly bathroom).

At the end of a party in a Mexican home, the host is apt to urge people to stay, no matter how late the hour. Once again, generosity and hospitality may take priority over sincerity. If the hour is late and the host looks exhausted, guests should probably take their leave, even if the host suggests they stay longer.

Hospitality on the Street

The values of hospitality and generosity extend beyond the home. The practice of Dutch treat is not common in Mexico. If one person in a group of friends says, "I'd like to invite you to a café for a Coke or coffee," the others assume that person will pay. Again, the word *invitar* (to invite) is the key. In these cases, the person who invites essentially takes on the role of host or hostess, and therefore takes full responsibility for paying for the others. Perhaps for this reason, separate checks in Mexican restaurants are a rarity.

In recent years the concept of Dutch treat has begun to take hold in some circles, particularly among groups of university students and young professionals. Even so, everyone present likes to appear as generous as possible. This might mean paying for a friend who has no change or picking up the tip. Most Mexicans would rather pay a little more and continue the conversation than to fuss over numbers. Splitting hairs over the bill would be considered cheap and in poor taste.

Even on the street, a well-bred Mexican generally does not buy anything to eat or drink, for example an ice cream cone, without inviting others in the group to the same treat. If an individual pulls out a cigarette, he first offers one to everyone else in the group. Regrettably, this custom is beginning to change as the economy worsens and as Mexicans become increasingly Americanized.

Sometimes Americans in Mexico complain that their Mexican hosts will never let them pay for anything, no matter how hard they try. The answer to this dilemma is to take the initiative and invite the hosts on another occasion.

Generosity: A Way of Life

Whether Mexicans are opening their home to guests or simply inviting friends out for a drink or snack, they instinctively follow unspoken codes of behavior for hosts and guests. These long-standing "rules" of hospitality, though, are by no means mere formulas or ritual. Rather, the generosity of most Mexicans reflects deeper values. In a culture where interdependence is valued above independence and human relationships matter more than material comforts, most Mexicans sense intuitively that it is more blessed to give than to receive. By sharing whatever they have, Mexicans enrich their own lives through deeper and more genuine human relationships.

Americans in Mexico are often struck by the extreme generosity of the Mexican people. One American college student wrote the following at the end of her one-month family homestay in the state of Veracruz:

> The most important thing that I have learned here is about giving my best to other people. For example, my (Mexican) mom liked my favorite shirt and normally I wouldn't want to give it away because it was my favorite. But now I realize that it is more important to make other people happy. The generosity here is incredible. . . . Because of my wonderful Mexican family, I feel that I have improved as a person. I feel that Mexico has helped me to overcome the "I'm out for me" concept and focus more on helping others.[1]

---

[1] Jennifer Kucer, final examination for Mexican Culture and Civilization course (Clemson University Summer Study Program in Xalapa, Veracruz, Mexico, June 1990), 3.

Mealtime

A Daily Highlight

For Mexicans, mealtime represents much more than physical nour-ishment. Over a leisurely multi-course meal, family members share thoughts, feelings, and ideas as well as good food. The main meal of the day, usually served around 2:30, is a daily highlight.

An American student summarized the importance of mealtime for Mexicans as follows:

> My Mexican family spent at least two hours together at the dinner table per day. I think that I became a member of my (host) family while sitting at that table. They asked me about the United States, told me about customs in Mexico and included me in their "inside jokes.". . . At the table Mexicans satisfy their need for companionship, love and respect as well as physical hunger. . . . I was so influenced by the closeness and joviality in my Mexican family, that I plan to attempt to introduce a more personal get-together time for my family at home.[1]

Not all families can spend two hours a day at the dinner table, but whenever possible, Mexicans like to take ample time to savor and enjoy a meal. Why rush on to something else if this time of family togetherness is so pleasant and the food is so tasty?

From the Río Grande to Yucatán: Much More than Tortillas

During their leisurely mealtime, Mexicans enjoy a cuisine that is

---

[1]Susan Gallop, final examination for Mexican Culture and Civilization course (Clemson University Summer Study Program in Xalapa, Veracruz, Mexico, June 1990), 2.

infinitely varied. The familiar menu of enchiladas, tacos, tamales, and chiles that one finds in "Mexican" restaurants throughout the United States comes originally from the desert regions on both sides of the Texas-Mexico border, hence the name Tex-Mex. These foods have become popular in all regions of Mexico as a light lunch or supper, especially in informal restaurants called *taquerías* (literally, taco places). Curiously, the ever-popular nachos found in many United States restaurants are an American invention; most Mexicans have never heard of them.

Farther south of the border, Mexico's rich variety of climate and topography allows for cultivation of abundant vegetables and tropical fruits. Cattle raising in the interior accounts for fine beef. Chicken, introduced by the Spanish conquistadors, is popular throughout Mexico. Both coasts offer all kinds of fish and other seafood. In Aztec times the noble class enjoyed fresh fish brought by runners from the Gulf. Today, particularly in the state of Veracruz and throughout the Yucatán peninsula, one finds a wide variety of seafood, including red snapper (*huachinango*), grouper (*mero*), shrimp (*camarones*), and lobster (*langosta*).

The cuisine of the Yucatán peninsula is quite distinctive, reflecting the Mayan heritage of the region as well as Yucatán's geographical isolation from the rest of the country. Yucatecan food is characterized by abundant fish, shellfish, chicken, and pork. In many ways it bears a closer resemblance to the food of Cuba and other Caribbean islands than to most Mexican cuisine. The most characteristic dishes of Yucatán, like those of Cuba and Puerto Rico, are less spicy than in other parts of Mexico. On the other hand, for those who like it hot, the hottest chile of all, the *chile habanero* (Havana chile) may be found in Yucatán.

Within all this variety, the most basic food staple is corn, or maize. In fact, the sacred book of the Mayas, the *Popol Vuh*, relates that man was created by the gods from *masa* (corn meal). For millions of Mexicans of all social and economic classes, the soft corn tortilla serves as the daily bread.

Almost as popular are the native frijoles (black or brown beans), which many families eat as an accompaniment to all meals including breakfast. Other foods indigenous to Mexico include several varieties of squashes, cacao (chocolate), numerous tropical fruits such as the mango, and an astonishing variety of chiles.

All these foods were familiar to the indigenous peoples of the area long before the arrival of the Spaniards. For pre-Columbian peoples of Mexico, the daily diet was essentially vegetarian: corn, beans, fruit, and vegetables. The conquering Spanish introduced domestic animals (chicken, beef, and pork), as well as rice, wheat, and many fruits previously unknown in the Americas. The rich variety of food that comprises Mexican cuisine today reflects the blending of the two cultures.

It is in the rural areas and small villages that today's diet most closely resembles that of pre-Columbian times. Here, despite the addition of chicken and pork, soft corn tortillas and frijoles remain the staples. In larger cities, the diet is more varied, reflecting a greater level of buying power and sophistication.

Contrary to popular belief, not all Mexican food is spicy, or *picante*. In most homes, chile sauces are presented on the side as condiments, as an option for those who like it hot. The most common are the *salsa roja* (red sauce) made from red chiles and the fiery *salsa verde* (green sauce). The degree to which food is *picante* varies greatly from one region to another, with the states of Oaxaca and Puebla vying for the claim to the spiciest food. Other popular seasonings throughout Mexico include cilantro (coriander), lime juice, all tomato sauces, and *achiote*, a tasty red seasoning similar to paprika.

Some traditional Mexican dishes include a blend of flavors that may initially surprise the Anglo-American palate. Most notably, the famous *mole* sauce (pronounced mo-lay) is a complex blend of chocolate, chiles, nuts, and spices to be served over meat, particularly chicken and turkey. While Anglo-Americans may initially express incredulity at the idea of seasoning meat with chocolate, those who stay in Mexico for any length of time usually acquire a taste for this unique culinary specialty. The recipes for *mole* and several other of the most characteristic Mexican dishes are the direct heritage of pre-Columbian cultures.

Daily Eating Patterns

The first meal of the day for a Mexican is not elaborate. Breakfast nearly always includes fresh fruit, especially in the more tropical regions in the southeast. Fruit may be served in almost any form. Especially popular are *licuados*, made by liquefying pieces of fruit in the blender and adding milk or cream, and *aguas* (literally, waters), a mixture of liquefied fruit and water. The more tropical the climate, the greater variety of fruits are available. A hearty breakfast might also include eggs, ham or steak, enchiladas with white cheese or cream on top, soft corn tortillas, and the ever-present frijoles.

Terms for the various meals each day vary according to region, just as meals in the United States might be called "breakfast, lunch, and dinner" or "breakfast, dinner, and supper." *Almuerzo* (literally, lunch) may refer to a heavy late breakfast or an early lunch.

Comida (literally, food, or dinner) refers to the principal meal of the day, whatever the hour. Most families gather for the *comida* between 2:00 and 3:00. This meal consists of several courses. First come homemade soup and pasta, then a meat or fish course with vegetables. These are followed by salad or fruit, possibly a dessert, and finally coffee. It is over coffee that most families linger for the delightful *sobremesa* (literally, over table), a time for relaxed conversation.

In restaurants as well as in the home, the *comida* is served at a more relaxed pace than in the United States. The waiter assumes that clients have come to enjoy and savor a meal, not to gulp down food as fast as possible. At the end of the meal, clients may remain at the table as long as they wish. With the exception of some restaurants with *comida rápida* (fast food), there is no pressure for clients to scurry off to make room for other diners. In fact, a well-trained Mexican waiter holds the bill until the client requests it. As long as no bill is presented, the clients may linger over coffee, just as if they were in the home of a friend.

The *merienda* (literally, snack) could be a late afternoon tea or a light supper as late as 10:00. In southeast Mexico, where the pace is more relaxed, a *merienda* around 6:00 or 7:00 can afford people an opportunity to get together for pleasant conversation. While businessmen get together in a local café for a beer, their wives might be entertaining women friends with a *merienda* at home. This could include coffee or soft drinks accompanied by something sweet such as pastry or cake. Naturally, as lifestyles become busier, as more women work outside the home, and as distances between homes of friends become greater, fewer and fewer Mexicans find time to sit down for this kind of *merienda*.

For most Mexicans, the final meal of the day is a light supper served around 9:00 or 9:30 in the evening. This evening *merienda* might consist of cereal, tacos, a sandwich, or *pan dulce* (sweet bread), accompanied by hot chocolate or coffee. Seldom do Mexicans eat a heavy meal at night, unless they go to a wedding or other special event. In this case the evening meal would be called a *cena* (supper).

Homemade is Best

For many Mexican women, especially in more traditional families, the preparation and presentation of the midday meal is a major daily activity. Women who work outside the home generally prefer to hire a maid to assist with the cooking rather than to present a skimpy or hastily prepared meal. Even when the maid does all the cooking, the lady of the house normally supervises menus and shopping.

Prepackaged foods are not popular in Mexico, and frozen dinners are almost nonexistent. Only in rare cases does a housewife resort to opening a can. Fresh ingredients are always preferred, including fresh spices when possible. Because high priority is given to fresh ingredients, shopping is frequent.

All medium-sized and large Mexican cities now have supermarkets similar to those found in the United States. A typical pattern might be to shop at the supermarket once a week and then, in addition, go to a neighborhood vegetable stand or butcher shop for fresh produce and meat almost daily. An abundance of produce stands and specialty shops in virtually every neighborhood facilitates this daily shopping. Large traditional markets are still found in every Mexican city, offering an astonishing variety of fresh produce.

With a philosophy of "waste not, want not," Mexicans tend to buy just enough for a meal. This way everything is fresh. The refrigerator is not likely to be filled with leftovers. A good Mexican housewife knows exactly what is in her refrigerator at any given moment.

Shopping for fresh produce every day may take a lot of time, especially if one needs to go to separate shops for vegetables, fruit, and meat. For most Mexicans, though, the pleasure of eating home-cooked food prepared from fresh ingredients outweighs any inconvenience concerning preparation time.

Leisure Time

Relaxing, Mexican Style

From the Mexican perspective, Anglo-Americans tend to spend their leisure time in a frenetic, even exhausting fashion. Some Americans may try to pack sight-seeing, travel, sports activities, and nightlife into one whirlwind vacation trip. How often do Americans exclaim, "I need a vacation to catch up on rest after my vacation!"

What does a Mexican do with his leisure time? Relax! Gather with friends at a sidewalk café. Cultivate the art of conversation. Share a poem, a song, a piece of philosophy. Savor a leisurely meal with family and close friends.

Mexicans do not postpone all their leisure to the weekend or the next major vacation; every day is ideally a healthy combination of work and relaxation. Business hours are spaced out to allow time to relax in the middle of each day. With morning business hours from 8:00 or 9:00 until 1:00 or 2:00, sidewalk cafés are usually crowded by 1:30. Around 2:00 or 2:30 most people return home for the leisurely main meal. (This is less true in Mexico City and other large cities, where travel time between work and home may be an hour or more.) For most Mexicans in provincial cities, the midday meal at home is followed by a leisurely time. The business day resumes at 4:00 and continues until about 8:00. Most government offices are open in the evening from 6:00 to 9:00. Since supper is not served until after 9:00, early evening is a popular time for window shopping, strolling, cruising (for upper-class teens), or chatting at sidewalk cafés.

Plazas, Parks, and Sidewalk Cafés

Like other Hispanics, Mexicans spend much more of their leisure time on city streets than do most people in the United States. Downtown streets in most Mexican cities bustle with shoppers, street vendors, and people watchers. Shopping malls on the outskirts of most Mexican cities are rapidly gaining popularity, especially among young people and suburbanites. Even so, the central business district remains busy and appealing. Around the central plaza or *zócalo* of every Mexican city, Mexicans watch the world go by. Mexican visitors to the United States often comment that city streets seem disconcertingly empty.

In the United States, one often hears, "My home is my castle." After a hard day at the office, the American executive may hurry home to an air-conditioned home, a cocktail, or television. By contrast, the Mexican businessman is much more likely to go to a favorite sidewalk café, where he can gather with friends, discuss events of the world, enjoy a cappuccino or a cold beer, and watch the world go by. While Mexican women may also be seen at the sidewalk cafés, many from the middle and upper classes prefer to meet in tea salons or elegant restaurants in the late afternoon for coffee and a rich dessert.

Ever popular are Sunday family outings to the nearest park or plaza. Mexico City's famous Chapultepec Park, the Mexican equivalent of New York City's Central Park, is a delightful spot to observe Mexicans at play. Every Sunday, Mexican families bearing large picnic baskets stream into Chapultepec. Inside the park are balloon vendors, marimba players, a lake with paddleboats, puppet shows, and vendors selling everything from hot dogs and ice cream to imported windup toys; all provide a colorful spectacle for the delight of Mexicans and visitors of all ages.

Television and Movies

Also popular on Sunday afternoons are nationally televised soccer matches. Many Mexican wives complain that they cannot tear their husbands and sons away from Sunday afternoon soccer, whether they watch it at home or at their favorite café or cantina. Sunday afternoon soccer is at least as popular in Mexico as Sunday afternoon football in the United States. Indeed, as a spectator sport, soccer is Mexico's national passion. When the World Cup soccer games were held in Mexico in 1986, millions of Mexicans of all social classes were glued to television sets in hotel lobbies, cafés, bars, and stores.

Sunday afternoon soccer is just one example of how television is changing patterns of social interaction throughout Mexico. Two decades ago, the cinema drew Mexicans like a magnet. In recent years, television and videocassette recorders have made a considerable dent in movie attendance and have kept more Mexicans at home in the evenings. The more remote the village, the greater the impact of television. In small villages, instead of going to the plaza to chat in the afternoon, women tend to gather in front of a neighbor's TV set.

In indigenous villages far from the national mainstream, television has become a high-priority item. In January 1987 the Mayan community of Muna, Yucatán (population 15,000), had only one telephone, no banks, and few toilets. Yet more than half the homes had television, and six had VCRs. By spring 1990 there were enough VCR owners in Muna to support two video rental stores, yet there was still only one telephone in the whole town.[1]

Throughout Mexico, among all social classes, Mexican-produced soap operas are among the most popular television programs. Most of these serialized stories, or *telenovelas*, portray glamorous wealthy Mexicans with liberal sexual mores and lives full of intrigue. Many episodes deal with the family stress caused by changing values and lifestyles of young, socially mobile Mexicans. The Mexican television industry, the largest and most successful in all Latin America, exports many of its programs to Spain and Central and South America. The Mexican government has occasionally used soap operas to shape public opinion, most notably to promote the concept of family planning and to warn of the dangers of drug and alcohol abuse.

Television shows from the United States account for about one third of all programming in Mexico. Most popular are those programs that show glamorous, rich Americans ("Dallas," "Dynasty") or clever law enforcement agents ("Miami Vice"). For better or worse, these programs do much to shape Mexican stereotypes about life in the United States.

Despite television and VCRs, movie theaters are still popular, especially for couples out on a date. American movies with subtitles draw the most viewers; first-run American films appear in Mexico City almost as soon as they are released and in smaller cities, anywhere from one to six months later. Mexican movies also have a great following; the Mexican film industry is the largest and most sophisticated in Latin America. Ever popular with the older generation are romantic films with glamorous stars and comedies with the famous Mexican comedian Cantinflas. Most young people, however, scorn these traditional stars, preferring films from the United States with Spanish subtitles. The younger generation also enjoys video games at home or in video parlors.

Weekend Entertainment

Mexicans enjoy live entertainment, be it a guitarist, a small-town comedian, a major symphony orchestra, or a theatrical production.

---

[1]Heusinkveld, "Muna Yucatán," 8.

Even in the smallest towns, many restaurants and bars offer live guitar music or a small band on Friday and Saturday nights. Mexicans dig deeper into their pockets than do most Anglo-Americans to pay for live music. Even a poor family will make every effort to hire musicians for a special event. One Mexican who could barely afford to eat paid $50 U.S. to hire a guitarist for his mother's birthday.

Mexicans love to dance. At most wedding receptions, *quinceaños* parties, and sometimes saint's day festivities, Mexicans of all ages crowd the dance floor to the strains of live music, often until the wee hours of the morning. An elderly great-grandmother may sway to the music in her wheelchair, while toddlers step to the music as they learn to walk. Disco dancing is the rage among Mexican teenagers and is also popular with many adults.

The larger the city, the greater variety of weekend entertainment is available. The entertainment section of most Mexican newspapers is much larger than in American cities of comparable size. Nightclub revues, live music, and floor shows at major hotels have broad appeal. In the largest cities, Mexicans who can afford it enjoy cultural offerings such as symphony orchestra concerts and live theater.

Sports: From Soccer to Bullfights

Weekends are also the time for organized sports. As a participation sport, soccer is to many Mexicans what baseball is for people in the United States. Most Mexican universities have intramural and competitive soccer teams; businesses and companies often organize adult teams for friendly competition. Children of middle- and upper-class families may join private soccer clubs, though on a much smaller scale than Little League baseball in the United States, since uniforms and equipment are expensive.

While news about soccer usually dominates the front page of any sports section, it is by no means the only sport of interest. Baseball and softball are also popular, and basketball is gaining in popularity. Regional and national competitions in swimming, track, and tennis attract middle- and upper-class children. As in the United States, Mexican sports teams are often named after animals such as pumas, tigers, lions, or cubs. However, Mexican sports teams never bear the name of any ethnic group (e.g., Redskins, Braves, Indians).

Mexicans are not as likely as people in the United States to engage in heavy physical exercise during their leisure time. For the most part, Mexicans have not been as preoccupied as Anglo-Americans with high cholesterol or elevated blood pressure. Patterns are changing, though, as one sees more and more Mexicans running daily and watching their diet. Programs such as aerobics, now available in most cities, are rapidly gaining in popularity.

In many small towns in the provinces, the "sport" that inspires the most passion is cockfighting. Usually held during state or local fairs, cockfights attract many spectators, especially from the lower classes. These spectacles are generally associated with heavy betting, drinking, and a rough crowd.

Bullfighting, imported from Spain, is considered more a pageant than a sport. Bullfights in Mexico City attract the most attention, both live and on television. Outside the capital, interest in bullfighting varies, depending to some degree on the availability of bulls. In Yucatán, where cattle raising is important, even the tiniest villages have bullfights on feast days and other special occasions. In some other regions, bullfights are practically nonexistent.

Vacation: Time to Relax

Vacations generally coincide with major holidays, with Christmas and Holy Week (Easter) being the most important. At these times, Mexico City becomes half empty as city dwellers head for the beaches or for visits with relatives in provincial cities. To a greater degree than other Mexicans, those who dwell in the congested capital feel the psychological need for a change of pace.

As Mexicans flock to their hometowns to be with their families during the holidays, business and government services in many cities almost come to a standstill. Throughout Mexico, many services such as plumbing, carpentry, or car repair are nearly impossible to obtain during holiday seasons. Major surgery may be postponed if the case is not too urgent.

At the beach, urban Mexicans enjoy the waves and the fresh air, but most try to avoid the direct rays of the sun. In a country where dark skin means either Indian ancestry or a life of toil in the fields, light skin is coveted. Tanning lotion is expensive, since foreigners are practically its only consumers.

While luxury resorts such as Cancún have become fashionable for very wealthy Mexicans, particularly those from the capital, the vast majority cannot afford even a brief stay. Day trips to nearby public beaches or other scenic spots are popular with many Mexicans; other families choose to relax close to home.

Unlike people in the United States who speak of getting back to nature, Mexicans show little interest in camping or vacationing in the wilderness. The idea of roughing it has little appeal in Mexico, a country where a significant percentage of the population live in substandard conditions year-round. There are many attractive national parks in Mexico, but almost no campgrounds.

In smaller cities and towns, where the pace of life is already relaxed and every day includes some leisure hours, most Mexicans do not feel the need to rush to a faraway vacation spot. For those Mexicans who choose to relax near home, leisure time remains just that. Enjoying a good meal with family and friends, discussing the events of the world over a cold beer at a sidewalk café, or sitting in the plaza to watch the world go by are all extremely satisfying. In a popular toast imported from Spain, Mexicans continue to raise their glasses to "health, wealth, love, and time to enjoy them!"

Holidays

A Fiesta for Every Occasion

Mexicans celebrate more holidays per year than practically any other culture. The blend of Hispanic and indigenous cultures has given Mexico an abundance of religious holidays and traditions. A colorful national history has provided the inspiration for numerous patriotic holidays. In addition, Mexicans have created secular holidays to honor practically everyone. On these special days, Mexicans leave their daily routine to worship, to celebrate, and to commemorate great moments in their nation's history.

To enjoy even more festivities, many Mexicans often arbitrarily create a *puente* (bridge), to make one holiday stretch into another. For example, in early May there are four holidays in quick succession: Labor Day (May 1), the Battle of Puebla (May 5), Mother's Day (May 10), and Teacher's Day (May 15). For many Mexicans, these offer an ideal framework for one extended holiday.

Catholic Holidays

Since Mexico is a Catholic country, all Christian holidays are important. Christmas season begins on December 12, the Day of the Virgin of Guadalupe. This is an official national holiday, with religious processions and special masses in many cities. Curiously, the day honoring the beloved Virgin of Guadalupe "happens" to correspond with an important Aztec holy day that was observed long before the arrival of the Spaniards in the sixteenth century.

For nine days preceding Christmas, many Mexicans still observe the traditional *posadas* (literally, inns). This custom, a symbolic reenactment of Mary and Joseph's search for lodging in Bethlehem, somewhat resembles the American custom of going caroling. A group of friends goes from house to house requesting lodging by means of a special carol and being refused, since there is "no room at the inn." At the last house, the hosts recognize the carolers as Mary, Joseph, and their entourage, and invite the group in for a party.

On Christmas Eve, many Mexicans attend midnight mass, known as *misa de gallo* (literally, rooster's mass). A meal with family and friends may follow immediately after mass, around midnight. Small gifts may be exchanged. Christmas Day is traditionally a leisurely time; in many homes this day is mostly devoted to napping, following Christmas Eve festivities.

Christmas season continues until Kings' Day (Epiphany) on January 6, the day when the three wise men are supposed to have arrived in Bethlehem. Most Mexican children still receive their most important gifts on January 6, from the *reyes magos* (wise men), despite the recent surge in popularity of Santa Claus, who appears with small gifts in many homes on December 24.

On Kings' Day many Mexican families serve their friends a special cake, the *rosca de reyes*. A tiny doll representing the infant Jesus is hidden inside the cake. Tradition demands that the guest who finds the doll inside his or her piece of cake must offer a party on February 2, forty days after Christmas, on the day known as *Candelaria*. This is the day when Mary and Joseph are supposed to have taken the baby Jesus to the temple for the first time.

The season of Lent begins with *Carnaval*, like Mardi Gras in New Orleans. The festivities associated with *Carnaval* vary greatly. Many cities, especially Veracruz and Mazatlán, have large parades with floats, costumes, and beauty queens.

Semana Santa (Holy Week) lasts for the entire week preceding Easter and often for one week afterward. Holy Week processions in some cities feature floats depicting various aspects of the passion of Christ. Maundy Thursday and Holy Friday are legal holidays, and most businesses and banks are closed. Perhaps ironically in a strongly Catholic country, Mexicans migrate to the beaches in droves during these days.

Saint's Days

The Catholic liturgical calendar has a saint's day for virtually every day of the year. Saint's days are generally more important than birthdays. Everyone named José celebrates the Day of Saint Joseph (March 19), all the Pablos, Paulos, Paulas, and Paulinas celebrate the Day of Saint Paul (June 29), and so forth. Even Mexicans with indigenous pagan names such as Cuauhtémoc generally have a Christian middle name so that they can observe a saint's day.

Almost all Mexicans, including non-practicing Catholics, celebrate their saint's day; no one wants to miss the fun of a party. Celebration of a saint's day usually includes a dinner or party with friends and family, plus a few gifts. The Mexican "Happy Birthday" song, *Las Mañanitas*, is actually a song for saint's days.

In addition to saint's days for individuals, nearly every town and city in Mexico has its patron saint. In many cities, a church may be dedicated to a particular saint. The smaller and more provincial the town, the greater is the importance given to the fiesta for the patron saint. Some small villages may spend almost their entire municipal budget on fiestas.

In his masterful essay on the Mexican fiesta, Nobel prize-winning writer Octavio Paz describes the psychology of letting go, of celebrating with exuberance. The Mexican fiesta, he maintains, provides an important psychological release from the cares of daily living. In the tiniest villages, people set aside their troubles for one glorious day of festivity, to live for the moment. The more dreary one's daily existence, the more one looks forward to the emotional release of a village fiesta.[1]

The Blend of Christian and Pagan Traditions

In the United States, holiday festivities include some secular or pagan elements from various European cultures (Christmas trees, the Easter bunny, Easter eggs). In Mexico, Santa Claus has become popular just in the past two decades. The Easter bunny, however, has not caught on, nor have Easter eggs.

Not surprisingly, major Catholic holidays in Mexico include elements from pre-Columbian indigenous tradition. The pre-Columbian influence is most notable on the Day of the Dead, celebrated throughout Mexico on November 1 and November 2. On the night of November 1 (All Saints' Day on the Catholic calendar), the souls of dead children are supposed to return to earth. Adult souls are awaited on the following night, November 2, or All Souls' Day.

The Day of the Dead in Mexico is a unique combination of indigenous and Catholic traditions. Many Mexican families make altars in their homes to honor their deceased relatives. These altars include flowers, usually marigolds, a photo of the deceased family member, and food or drink that the dead person liked.

Mexicans also observe this special day by visiting the graves of ancestors, often taking a picnic to the grave site. Many families have a reunion while cleaning the tombstone and dressing it with flowers or other ornaments. Other families take candles and keep watch all night.

Images of death are everywhere. Stores sell sugar candy skulls,

---

[1]Octavio Paz, *The Labyrinth of Solitude*, 47-64.

and bakeries make skull-shaped pastries. The tone of this holiday is generally festive, giving some foreign visitors the impression that Mexicans must be morbid or insensitive to death. In fact, Mexicans simply confront the concept of death more openly than do most Anglo-Americans. Whereas many people in the United States feel uncomfortable with the subject of death, Mexicans, with their sugar skulls and coffins, make fun of death; they accept the idea that death is a natural part of the life cycle.

Secular Holidays, Family Days

Mexicans celebrate a special day for practically everyone: Mother's Day, Father's Day, Child's Day, Teacher's Day, Lawyer's Day, Architect's Day, and more. Because of the tremendous importance of motherhood in Mexican culture, Mother's Day (May 10) is by far the most important of these holidays. On the day preceding Mother's Day, bus stations are jammed with adults en route to their hometowns to spend the day with their mother. Absenteeism on the job is high on Mother's Day, and many businesses simply close. Long-distance lines are jammed as Mexicans telephone their mothers from as far away as Europe and Asia. Nearly all working mothers, including teachers and other professionals, are excused from work that day. In addition to cards, flowers, congratulations, and perhaps a meal out, mothers may receive major gifts such as a new refrigerator or television. There are also large pilgrimages to cemeteries to lay flowers on the mother's grave.

On other holidays such as Father's Day, Child's Day, and Teacher's Day, Mexicans honor people with flowers, gifts, embraces, and compliments. Special programs in city plazas feature music, entertainment, and flowery speeches in praise of the honorees.

Some minor holidays in the United States of secular or forgotten origin (e.g., April Fools' Day) retain religious significance in Mexico. The Hispanic equivalent of April Fools' Day is the *Día de los Inocentes* (Day of the Innocent Ones) on December 28, in commemoration of Herod's slaying of babies. Since the word *inocente* in Spanish also means "naive," practical jokes are numerous. When a Mexican falls for a joke, his friend says *Pasaste por inocente* ("You passed for a naive, innocent one").

Patriotic Celebrations

Patriotic holidays commemorate great moments in Mexican national history. They honor neither the Aztec tradition nor moments in the Spanish conquest, but rather crucial events in the making of modern Mexico. The most important include Independence Day (September 16), commemorating Father Hidalgo's first cry for Mexican independence from Spain in 1810; the *Cinco de Mayo* (literally, May 5 Day), marking the Mexican victory over French forces at the Battle of Puebla in 1862; and the Day of the Revolution (November 20), commemorating the beginning of the Mexican Revolution in 1910. Also very important is Labor Day, or the International Day of the Worker (May 1).

Other patriotic holidays for which most stores and banks are closed include the Day of the 1917 Constitution (February 5); Flag Day (February 24); Benito Juárez's birthday (March 21); and the Day of the Oil Expropriation (March 18), commemorating the 1938 expropriation by the Mexican government of all foreign-owned oil companies.

All these patriotic holidays are celebrated with a great deal of pomp. Festivities usually include processions of school children and various dignitaries, patriotic speeches, declamations of poetry, and a variety of programs extolling Mexico and the brave sacrifices of national heroes.

Labor Day is a much more important holiday in Mexico than in the United States. On the Day of the Worker on May 1, members of all *sindicatos* (labor unions) pass in uniform before municipal and state officials to the accompaniment of rousing music. The procession lasts for hours, since nearly all workers in Mexico are unionized. There are unions for nearly every profession, from bricklayers and taxi drivers to university professors and classical musicians. With practically everyone in the parade, it seems a wonder that there are spectators.

The well-known Mexican philosopher Samuel Ramos has theorized that Mexicans have so many patriotic holidays because they are insecure about the value of their nationality.[2] He argues that the patriotic speeches and other fanfare help to bolster Mexicans' confidence in their country, counteracting feelings that Mexico may not be as good as other nations. Certainly, these celebrations do appeal to Mexicans' sense of national pride. Fervent poetical declamations about the glories of Mexico may actually move listeners to tears.

Nevertheless, Mexico's best-known philosopher, Octavio Paz, may come closer to the mark in explaining Mexico's many holidays. Simply, Mexicans enjoy a good party. A good Mexican fiesta provides a powerful emotional release from the often tenuous business of daily living. On the day of a fiesta, Mexicans succeed in setting aside their cares to enjoy the moment to the fullest. No matter how heavy one's work load or how mundane one's daily existence, Mexicans can always look forward to a holiday just ahead.

---

[2]Samuel Ramos, *Profile of Man and Culture in Mexico,* trans. Peter G. Earle (Austin: University of Texas Press, 1962), 63.

Art and Music
Beauty in Daily Life

In the United States, the word art is frequently understood to refer primarily to the fine arts—to those polished artistic creations that one might seek out in museums, theaters, or concert halls. With a practical, utilitarian outlook on life, too many Anglo-Americans tend to consider art as a luxury for the elite, for those who understand it and can afford it.

For Mexicans, art is an integral part of daily life. *Arte* in Mexico might refer to any of those things that add a sense of beauty, poetry, or dignity to an otherwise mundane existence. Mexicans of virtually all social classes enhance their daily life with color, flowers, music, and poetry. In Mexico, art is for everyone.

The Tradition of Handicraft

The tradition of fine *artesanía* (handicraft) in Mexico predates the Spanish conquest. When the Spaniards arrived in 1519, they found a rich tradition of Indian crafts, including ceramics, weavings, copper work, painted wood, onyx carvings, jewelry, and more. One enlightened priest of the sixteenth century, Padre Vasco de Quiroga, was so impressed with the handicrafts in what is now the western state of Michoacán that he imported master craftsmen from Spain to help the Indians improve their skills. With a utopian vision of non-competition, he cultivated a different craft specialty for each village in the region: copper work for the village of Santa Clara, painted lacquered wood for Pátzcuaro and Uruapan, cloth weavings for yet other villages, and so forth. Thanks to Padre Quiroga's foresight, Michoacán enjoys even now the reputation for producing the greatest variety of handicraft in Mexico. But virtually every Mexican state boasts its own craft specialties.

Each indigenous culture, ranging from the Yaqui Indians in the desert northwest to the Mayas of the Yucatán peninsula, has developed different crafts according to its particular needs and tastes. Crafts also vary according to the availability of native materials in different regions. The famous black pottery from Oaxaca, for example, is made from volcanic soils in valleys surrounding that city; textiles vary from one region to another according to the availability of fabrics and dyes.

Artisans may use any materials at hand to create an object of beauty. In the village of Tzintzuntzán in Michoacán, one old man passed the time by weaving thin reeds from nearby Lake Pátzcuaro into various designs. In the 1940s an American anthropologist took note of this man's skill and encouraged him to pass on his craft to younger artisans before he died. Thus a prosperous new craft industry was born; the entire town continues to be famous for its delicately woven straw objects.

This folk art is not just for ornamentation; rather, Mexican artisans add beauty to objects of daily use. In the simplest household, one might find hand-painted water jugs, colorful woven baskets, elaborately carved wooden kitchen utensils, painted wooden spoons, finely wrought copper kettles, and hand-embroidered clothing. In recent years, however, these objects have been relegated more and more to decorative ornaments; teflon and rayon are making life easier for the housewife.

Color is perhaps the most important element of Mexican folk art, more eye-catching than form, shape, or line. In towns and cities throughout Mexico, one sees houses painted in brilliant shades of pink, yellow, blue, and green. Inside the most modest homes, there are brightly colored handwoven blankets, embroidered tablecloths, place mats, and even dish towels.

Flowers, too, add color to daily life. Especially in tropical areas, lush flowering trees in almost every yard can transform the most humble village into a wonderland of color. Floral arrangements— whether they be real or made from paper, yarn, or fabric—adorn Mexican homes of all classes.

From Mariachis to Marimbas

The visual arts are just one way that Mexicans brighten their daily existence. Perhaps even more essential to their sense of well-being is music. One might think that Mexicans are born dancing. The smallest toddlers learn to dance at family gatherings, swaying and stepping in time to the music to the delight of older relatives.

No party is complete without a guitar and singing, and nearly every Mexican seems to have some notion of how to play the guitar. Virtually all Mexicans seem to know the lyrics to a large body of traditional songs. These songs are so common at family gatherings and fiestas that children learn them almost unconsciously. Consequently, even though the teens have their own music, there is not such a generation gap in musical taste as one often finds in the United States.

Music varies widely from region to region. The traditional *mariachis,* those musicians with huge sombreros and elaborately embroidered outfits, come originally from the western state of Jalisco, around the city of Guadalajara. The word *mariachi* derives from the French word *mariage* (marriage). During the time of the French occupation of Mexico in the 1860s, Mexican musicians were asked to perform at weddings and other elegant parties of the French. From this period developed the now familiar repertoire of *mariachi* music.

A typical *mariachi* group consists of anywhere from five to fifteen musicians playing trumpets, violins, and guitars. The lively, upbeat music of the *mariachis* may sometimes sound raucous to foreign ears, especially with the penetrating sound of the trumpets. For Mexicans, though, this music expresses the zest of living. The lyrics, usually romantic, are much more expressive and poetic than those of most pop hits in the United States. In fact, the lyrics of some songs are taken directly from the works of the best known poets. Mexicans living in the United States often listen to *mariachi* music at high volume on tapes or radio, in part to maintain a connection with their own culture while they dwell in a foreign land.

In tropical regions in southeastern Mexico, trumpets and violins give way to harps and marimbas. The famous *"La Bamba,"* originally played on the harp, reflects the exuberance and gaiety of the *jarochos*, the people from Veracruz. Farther south, in the states of Tabasco and Chiapas and throughout the Yucatán peninsula, music tends to be sweeter and more lilting. The gentler rhythms seem appropriate for the tropical climate, where every aspect of life moves slowly.

Poetry for Everyone

The poetry of music is so compelling for Mexicans that recitation of poetry itself has become an art form. In provincial towns throughout Mexico, a typical summer band concert in the plaza is likely to include several selections of poetic declamation. The more effusive and melodramatic the recitation, the more enthusiastic is the applause. When a poem is especially romantic, some listeners may actually be moved to tears.

This love of poetry even carries over into Mexican bars. A guitarist with a good voice and poetic lyrics can quickly draw an appreciative group of admirers in any bar or café. Typically, a client might ask the guitarist, "Could you play some background accompaniment so that I can recite a poem?" Such a request is always honored, and the poem, whether well recited or not, is sure to be received with warm applause and exclamations of approval. Sometimes a guitar may be accompanied by impromptu lyrics gently spoofing one of the patrons. Such musical gatherings may last long into the night, or even into the early hours of dawn. On occasions like this, music and poetry weave a magical spell that binds strangers together and enriches the lives of those who listen.

Folkloric Dances

Even more varied than the music itself are the folkloric dances from each region. Virtually every state has its own dances, often deriving from indigenous tradition. These dances range from the stark Yaqui Deer Dance from the desert northwest, an artistic reenactment of the hunt, to the exuberant *bamba* from Veracruz.

Mexicans throughout the country continue to enjoy traditional regional dances at festivals and on feast days. In addition, the most representative dances of each state have been codified and are now taught in every school and even in university classes. In Mexico City, in the elegant settings of the Palace of Fine Arts and the National Theater of Mexico, tourists see stylized versions of ancient dances at the famous Ballet Folklórico, a stunning production with magnificent costumes and musicians that has won worldwide acclaim and international prizes. The University of Veracruz in Xalapa has another Ballet Folklórico which has also received wide acclaim abroad.

Indigenous Motifs and the Fine Arts

In the professional Ballet Folklórico, what began as native rain dances and folkloric rituals of courtship have been elevated to the status of high culture. This is just one example of Mexicans' recognition of the unique artistic value of their Indian heritage. But this realization did not come easily.

Before the great Mexican Revolution of 1910, upper-class Mexicans tried to ignore their country's Indian roots. Painters and writers imitated French romanticism and other European models, since indigenous themes and motifs were not considered worthy subjects for fine art. Even the great pre-Columbian art treasures of Mexico were viewed with relative indifference.

The Revolution resulted in a new cultural awareness of Mexico's own artistic roots and an outpouring of creative imagination. The

Mexican Indian became the favorite theme of painters, sculptors, poets, novelists, and essayists. Especially noteworthy are the great mural painters—Diego Rivera, José Clemente Orozco, and David Siqueiros—whose murals portray the Indians and the poor as the most sympathetic figures of Mexican history. Ironically, in government buildings of Spanish colonial style, bold murals by these and other artists depict graphically the cruel treatment of the Indians by the conquering Spanish. These murals have served to give Mexicans of all social classes an increased awareness of, and pride in their own history.

A National Patrimony for All Mexicans

With the Mexican Revolution came also an increased appreciation of the glories of Mexico's pre-Columbian art. The most outstanding of these treasures may now be found in the National Museum of Anthropology in Mexico City, opened in 1964 and judged by many to be the best of its kind in the world. Here, thanks to a policy of reasonable admission fees and free admission on Sundays, Mexicans of all social classes may join visitors from around the world to admire the monumental statues, stone carvings, codices, gold jewelry, and innumerable other artifacts of several dozen pre-Columbian cultures. In addition, nearly every state in Mexico has an excellent regional museum. Especially noteworthy is the Museum of Anthropology in Xalapa, Veracruz.

The same policy of trying to make the arts accessible to everyone has generally applied to these regional museums and to archaeological sites throughout the country. Primary school children take excursions to museums two or three times a year. Thus, Mexicans of all socioeconomic classes can gain an appreciation and knowledge of their national heritage.

In regions with a high percentage of Indian population, upper-class Mexicans have traditionally eschewed the folk art of today's Indians. This attitude reflects an ever-present contradiction in Mexican thought: the tendency to glorify Mexico's Indian past and to look down upon Indian cultures of today. In recent years, however, native handicraft has become more fashionable. In the city of Mérida, Yucatán, for example, upper-class women have recently started buying the traditional *huipil* dresses of the Mayas. Ironically, just as Indians have begun to exchange their traditional embroidered dresses for cheap ready-made clothes, upper-class women have come to appreciate the practicality of these loose white cotton garments for a tropical climate.

Native handicraft has also been recognized at official levels for its artistic value. In provincial capitals around the country, museums of decorative arts feature the most exquisite handicraft of each region. This growing recognition of native handicraft as legitimate art represents one more step in coming to terms with Mexico's Indian past.

Art crosses socioeconomic boundaries and enriches the life of all Mexicans. Whether Mexicans are visiting the great archaeological sites of ancient civilizations, creating a poem, singing a romantic melody, or weaving a basket, they are constantly enhancing their lives with some form of art. Mexican writer Carlos Fuentes believes that the arts represent Mexico's greatest contribution to world culture. He points out that the creative genius of the Mexicans manifests itself not so much in technological advances, scientific inventions, or democratic models, but in the arts: in pre-Columbian temples, in handicrafts, in bold mural paintings, in poetry, song, and dance. Mexicans seem to sense instinctively that art and music ennoble the human spirit and enrich the quality of life for everyone. In this regard, Anglo-Americans have much to learn from the Mexicans.

Conclusion

Becoming Better Neighbors

In this last decade of the twentieth century, Mexico and the United States are becoming closer neighbors than ever before. American culture spills over into Mexico by means of television, movies, popular music, and consumer products. Young urban Mexicans imitate American fashions and admire American sports heroes. American television programs send images of a fast-paced, materialistic lifestyle to far-flung Mexican villages.

At the same time, Mexican culture is increasingly evident in the United States. According to the 1990 census, the 12.5 million Mexicans and Mexican-Americans who reside legally within the United States comprise five percent of the population. Not surprisingly, Mexican culture is bringing new flavor to life north of the border. Society pages of many newspapers in Texas, Arizona, New Mexico, and southern California now regularly feature *quinceaños* parties, as fifteen-year-old Mexican-American girls celebrate their entry into society.

In East Los Angeles, enormous murals in bold colors portray heroes from Mexican history. Mexican-Americans in San Antonio observe Mexican Independence Day as a major holiday. Television stations throughout the Southwest continue to increase their Spanish language programming with Mexican soap operas, mariachi music, and news of Mexican sports teams. Two cable networks, Univisión and Telemundo, reach out to Hispanic viewers. Throughout the United States, Mexican foods such as tacos, burritos, and guacamole continue to gain in popularity.

In the next few years, with the ratification of the Free Trade Agreement between Mexico and the United States almost a certainty, we may expect the flow of culture in both directions to increase dramatically. As industrialists, businessmen, and consumers engage in more trade, people on both sides of the border will have unprecedented opportunities to learn from each other.

However, a cultural homogenization is neither desirable nor likely. The external, or surface elements of culture—foods, fashions, music—flow across national boundaries relatively easily. Deep-rooted values are not so easily transplanted or dislodged. Even as people from Mexico and the United States come to know each other better, the distinctive values, behaviors, customs, and attitudes that characterize each culture are likely to remain.

As the two countries become more interdependent, a new era of Mexican-American relations lies ahead. Whether increased contact will lead to greater mutual understanding will depend on good will on both sides. The stereotypes and cultural arrogance of the past must give way to respect for and appreciation of cultural differences.

Mexicans have much wisdom to offer their Anglo-American neighbors, as well as much to learn. Their philosophy of taking time to savor life, their ability to keep work and play in perspective, their deep appreciation of art and music, and their willingness to take the time to cultivate human relationships can provide valuable lessons for Anglo- Americans.

With respect and good will, both Anglo-Americans and Mexicans can enrich their lives through knowledge of the other. It is to be hoped that with greater mutual understanding, people on both sides of the border can become better neighbors. We need each other.

Basic Facts About Mexico[1]

THE LAND

Area: 760,300 square miles (1,972,546 square kilometers)

Elevation: Highest point: Citlatépetl, 18,696 ft.
Lowest point: sea level

Physical geography: Two great mountain ranges, the Sierra Madre Occidental in the west and the Sierra Madre Oriental in the east contain between them the central plateau, where most Mexicans live. In the north this central plateau averages between 3,000 and 5,000 ft. above sea level; in the south, around Mexico City, the plateau is from 7,000 to 9,000 ft. The western sierra, the higher of the two ranges, is rugged and precipitous, whereas the eastern sierra, like the Appalachians in the United States, is older and softer in appearance.

South of Mexico City, a third range of more recent volcanic origin runs east and west. Mexico's highest mountains, including Citlatépetl (or Pico de Orizaba) and the famous Popocatépetl (17,888 ft.) and Ixtaccíhuatl (17,343 ft.) are found here.

Mountains prevent adequate rainfall from arriving to the central plateau, creating semiarid conditions in most of the country. The driest region is northwestern Mexico, similar in topography and climate to the American southwestern states of Arizona and New Mexico. The eastern Mexican states bordering the Gulf of Mexico, by contrast, are lush, green, and tropical, watered by rains originating in the Gulf. Coffee, sugar, bananas, and ornamental flowers are the primary cash crops of the state of Veracruz.

The southernmost state of Chiapas on the border with Guatemala is characterized by lush, tropical rain forests and mountains rising to over 10,000 feet.

The Yucatán peninsula to the southeast is a nearly flat limestone shelf with tropical temperatures, scrubby vegetation, and famous white sand beaches such as those of Cancún and Cozumel.

Capital city: México D.F., 1992 population estimated 21 million

Major cities:	States where located:
Mexico City	D.F. (Federal District)
Guadalajara	Jalisco
Monterrey	Nuevo León
Puebla	Puebla
León	Guanajuato
Ciudad Juárez	Chihuahua
Tijuana	Baja California Norte
Aguascalientes	Aguascalientes
Mexicali	Baja California Norte
Culiacán	Sinaloa
Acapulco	Guerrero
Mérida	Yucatán
Chihuahua	Chihuahua
San Luis Potosí	San Luis Potosí
Morelia	Michoacán

THE PEOPLE

Population: 81,000,000 (1990)

Race:

Mestizo (blend of Spanish and Indian)	60%
Amerindian or predominantly Amerindian	30%
White or predominantly white	9%
Other	1%

Religion:

Roman Catholic	92.6%
Protestant	3.3%
Other	4.1%

Official language: Spanish, spoken by 95% of Mexicans

Major indigenous languages:

Nahuatl	(central Mexico)
Maya	(Yucatán peninsula)
Maya-Quiché	(state of Chiapas)
Zapotec	(valley of Oaxaca)
Mixtec	(valley of Oaxaca)

Major indigenous languages (cont.):

Tarascan	(state of Michoacán)
Otomí	(central Mexico)
Totonaco	(state of Veracruz)

There are over 50 recorded languages and over 500 recorded dialects in Mexico.

Literacy: 88% (1991)

Life expectancy: 68 years male, 76 years female (1990)

Mexicans and Mexican-Americans in U.S.: 12,565,000 (5% of U.S. population) (1990 legal residents)

Total Hispanics in U.S.: 20,076,000 (8% of U.S. pop.) (1990)

GOVERNMENT AND POLITICS

Official name of country: Estados Unidos Mexicanos (United Mexican States)

Political divisions: 31 states, plus Federal District (D.F.)

Form of government: Federal republic operating under a centralized government.

Constitution: February 5, 1917

Presidency: one six-year term, no reelection. Candidates are chosen from within each party. Since 1934, all presidents have been from the PRI (Institutional Revolutionary Party).
Presidents of Mexico since 1934:

Lázaro Cárdenas	1934-40
Manuel Avila Camacho	1940-46
Miguel Alemán	1946-52
Adolfo Ruiz Cortines	1952-58
Adolfo López Mateos	1958-64
Gustavo Díaz Ordaz	1964-70
Luis Echeverría	1970-76
José López Portillo	1976-82
Miguel de la Madrid	1982-88
Carlos Salinas de Gortari	1988-94

Major political parties:

PRI   (Institutional Revolutionary Party). In power since 1930s; completely dominates national politics. Pledges to uphold the Revolutionary Constitution of 1917. Every president since 1934 has been from the PRI, plus almost every governor. PRI controls the political center; it has won, bought, or co-opted the support of almost every important constituency, including labor unions, farmers, industrialists, the media, and business. PRI has traditionally had a particularly tight hold on labor unions.

PAN   (National Action Party). Politically to the right of PRI, the strongest opposition party until 1988. Supported by some conservative businessmen, traditional landed families, and conservative Catholic elements. Its strongest power base is in areas far from Mexico City with strong regional politics, especially the states of Chihuahua in the north and Yucatán in the southeast. PAN consistently wins a significant minority of seats in the National Chamber of Deputies and has won municipal elections in Yucatán, Chihuahua, and elsewhere, particularly in the north. Won the gubernatorial election in the state of Chihuahua in July 1992.

PRD   (Democratic Revolutionary Party). Rising party to the left of PRI. Gained broad support in 1988, especially among the *campesinos* (farmers) and the working classes, with the presidential candidacy of Cuauhtémoc Cárdenas, son of populist president of the 1930s, Lázaro Cárdenas. Many Mexicans believe that Cárdenas and the PRD actually won the 1988 presidential election. In July 1992 in Cárdenas's home state of Michoacán, the PRD officially lost a hotly contested gubernatorial election. The PRI-controlled press cited this as the beginning of the demise of the PRD, while the PRD pressed multiple charges of electoral fraud.

THE ECONOMY

Monetary unit: the Mexican peso
January 1, 1993: Introduction into circulation of the new Mexican peso. One new Mexican peso is equivalent to one thousand old Mexican pesos.

Primary products and industries:
petroleum (crude oil and oil products)
tourism
industry (steel, automobiles, chemicals, food and beverages, textiles)

Primary products and industries (cont.):
mining (silver, copper, lead, zinc)
agriculture (coffee, corn, cotton, sugar, tobacco, wheat)
fishing (shrimp)

Economic partners:

United States	66%
Europe	16%
Japan	11%
Other	7%

Per capita income:

Mexico:	$2,680 (1990)
United States:	$14,056 (1989)

CHRONOLOGY OF IMPORTANT EVENTS
IN MEXICAN HISTORY

Ca. 3000-2000 B.C.   Cultivation of corn begins.

Ca. 1000 B.C.   Olmec civilization flourishes along tropical Gulf Coast.

Ca. AD 600-900   Mayan culture reaches its peak in the Yucatán peninsula.

Ca. AD 1000-1100   Mayas and Toltecs build Chichén-Itzá in the Yucatán peninsula.

1325   Aztecs found their capital city of Tenochtitlán (now Mexico City).

1519   Conquistador Hernán Cortés lands on Mexican soil at Veracruz with five hundred Spanish soldiers.

1520   Spaniards drive the Aztecs from their capital in Tenochtitlán.

1521   Final defeat of the Aztec nation by Cortés's forces at the present site of the Plaza de Tlalteloco in Mexico City.

1521 - 1821   Mexico is a colony of Spain.

1523   Arrival of first Spanish monks.

Dec. 12, 1531   First appearance of the Virgin of Guadalupe to Juan Diego.

1533   Founding of the University of Mexico.

1535   Arrival of the first Spanish viceroy, Don Antonio de Mendoza. Mexico becomes the Viceroyalty of New Spain.

Sept. 16, 1810   First cry for independence from Spain by Padre Hidalgo in the small town of Dolores. The insurrection fails; Hidalgo is executed in 1811.

1821   Mexican independence is achieved, and a treaty is signed.

1822   Colonel Agustín de Iturbide, leader of the revolutionary insurgents, declares himself emperor of Mexico; he holds on to power for less than seven months.

1824   Mexico becomes a federal republic with nineteen states and four territories.

1833 - 1855   General Antonio López de Santa Anna dominates the Mexican political scene. He is elected president 11 times.

1835   Texas declares itself a republic.

1845   The United States annexes Texas.

1846 - 1848   Mexican-American War. The Treaty of Guadalupe Hidalgo cedes more than half of Mexico's national territory to the United States.

1853   The United States buys the Mesilla Valley (southernmost part of Arizona and New Mexico) from Mexico in the Gadsden Purchase.

1857   New liberal constitution diminishes the power of privileged groups, especially the Catholic Church.

1857 - 1861   The Laws of Reform, promulgated by Benito Juárez, officially separate church and state.

1862 - 1867   Interlude of foreign rule, known as the French Intervention.

May 5, 1862   The Battle of Puebla, in which Mexican forces defeat invading French forces. Mexicans celebrate this event as an official holiday every May 5 (*Cinco de Mayo*).

1864   Emperor Maximilian, brother of the Austrian emperor Franz Josef of the Hapsburg line, arrives with his wife Carlota to assume power of Mexico, in the name of Napoleon III.

1867   Maximilian is executed outside Querétaro.

1877 - 1910   Presidency of dictator Porfirio Díaz. Much economic and industrial progress at the expense of social justice and political freedom.

1910   Beginning of the Mexican Revolution. Candidate Francisco I. Madero challenges dictator Porfirio Díaz and demands honest elections.

1911   Madero is named president; Díaz flees Mexico.

1913   Madero is killed; Army chief Victoriano Huerta becomes
        president in a counterrevolution. Various revolutionary
        forces gather behind three separate leaders: Emiliano Zapata
        in the south, Francisco (Pancho) Villa in the north, and
        Venustiano Carranza, who appealed to the middle classes and
        intellectuals.

1914 - 1917   United States marines land in Veracruz, prepared to
        back Carranza forces. Carranza drives Zapata and Villa from
        the capital. Villa leads raids across the United States border.

Feb. 5, 1917   Carranza-backed constitution is approved; it is still in
        place today.

1924 - 1934   President Plutarco Elías Calles consolidates
        presidential power and forms a single national party, PRN
        (National Revolutionary Party).

1934 - 1940   Presidency of Lázaro Cárdenas; foundation of the
        PRI (Institutional Revolutionary Party) and the political
        system that is still in place. Much social legislation and
        redistribution of large land holdings.

Mar. 18, 1938   Expropriation of foreign oil companies.

1940 - 1946   Presidency of Avila Camacho. War is declared on the
        Axis powers.

1946 - 1952   Presidency of Miguel Alemán. Economic expansion,
        widespread corruption. Construction of the new main
        campus
        of the UNAM (Universidad Nacional Autónoma de México).

1953   Women's suffrage is granted.

1952 - 1958   Presidency of Adolfo Ruiz Cortines.

1958 - 1964   Presidency of Adolfo López Mateos.

1964 - 1970   Presidency of Gustavo Díaz Ordaz.

1968   Student protests coincide with holding of Olympic games in
        Mexico City. Confrontation at the Plaza of Tlalteloco in
        Mexico City, in which more than five hundred people, mostly
        students, were reported killed by Mexican police.

1970 - 1976   Presidency of Luis Echeverría. First devaluation of
        the Mexican peso since early 1950s. Active government
        stand on population control, with public health clinics and
        free contraceptives throughout Mexico.

1976 - 1982   Presidency of José López Portillo. Oil boom and
        crash. Widespread government corruption.

Aug. 1982   Economic crisis due to plummeting oil prices.
        Nationalization of all Mexican banks by President López
        Portillo.

1982 - 1988   President Miguel de la Madrid. Promises of
                crackdown on corruption.

Sep. 19, 1985   Major earthquake in Mexico City and several
                western cities (8.1 on the Richter scale). 4,200 fatalities
                reported.

1986   World Cup Soccer Games in Mexico.

1988   Rise of PRD (Democratic Revolutionary Party) on the left,
                under Cuauhtémoc Cárdenas. Widespread accusations of
                dishonest presidential election.

1988 - 1994   Presidency of Carlos Salinas de Gortari. Privatization
                of banks and some previously state-run industries. Promises
                for reforms within the PRI.

May 1992   Educational Reform Act transfers control of public
                education from the federal government to the states and raises
                the number of years of obligatory schooling from six to nine.

August 1992   Free Trade Agreement is signed by chief executives
                of Canada, the United States, and   Mexico.

OFFICIAL HOLIDAYS

January 1	New Year's Day
February 5	Day of the Constitution (1917)
February 24	Flag Day
March 18	Day of the Oil Expropriation (1938)
March 21	Benito Juárez's birthday (1806)
March/April	Maundy Thursday, Good Friday, Holy Saturday, Easter
May 1	Day of the Worker (Labor Day)
May 5	Battle of Puebla against the French (1862)
May 10	Mother's Day
September 16	Mexican Independence Day (1810)
October 12	Day of the Mestizo Race (Columbus Day)
November 1	Day of the Dead (All Saints' Day)
November 2	Day of the Dead (All Souls' Day)
November 20	Day of the Mexican Revolution (1910)
December 12	Our Lady of Guadalupe
December 25	Christmas

[1] Sources: Brian Hunter, ed., *The Statesman's Yearbook* (New York: St. Martin's Press, 1991), 864-870. *The Europa World Yearbook,* (London: Europa Publications, 1991), 1806-1829. *Statistical Abstract of the United States* (Washington, D.C.: U.S. Department of Commerce, Bureau of the Census, 1991), 385. *The World Factbook* (Washington, D.C.: Central Intelligence Agency, 1991), 204-206.

Selected Bibliography

Alba, Victor. *The Horizon Concise History of Mexico.* New York: American Heritage Publishing Co., 1973.

Bartra, Roger. *La jaula de la melancolía: Identidad y metamorfosis del mexicano.* Mexico City: Grijalbo, 1987.

Brandenburg, Frank. *The Making of Modern Mexico.* Englewood Cliffs, N.J.: Prentice-Hall, 1964.

Brenner, Anita. *The Wind That Swept Mexico.* Austin: University of Texas Press, 1971.

Burma, John, ed. *Mexican Americans in the United States: A Reader.* New York: Harper & Row, 1970.

Camp. Roderic A. *Politics in Mexico.* New York: Oxford University Press, 1993.

Condon, John C. *Good Neighbors: Communicating with the Mexicans.* Yarmouth, Maine: Intercultural Press, 1985.

Díaz Guerrero, Rogelio. *Psicología del mexicano.* 5th ed. Mexico City: Editorial Trillas, 1990.

Doring, María Teresa. *El mexicano ante la sexualidad.* Mexico City: Hispánicas, 1990.

Fehrenbach, T. R. *Fire and Blood: A History of Mexico.* New York: Macmillan, 1973.

Franz, Carl. *The People's Guide to Mexico.* Santa Fe, N.M.: John Muir Publications, 1974.

Gorden, Raymond L. *Living in Latin America: A Case Study in Cross-Cultural Communication.* Lincolnwood, Ill.: National Textbook Company, 1974.

Guillermoprieto, Alma. "Report from Mexico: Serenading the Future," *The New Yorker*, November 9, 1992, 96-104.

Heer, David M. *Undocumented Mexicans in the United States.* New York: Cambridge University Press, 1990.

Heusinkveld, Paula R. "Muna, Yucatan: A Mayan Village Enters the Mainstream" (Unpublished paper presented at the South Eastern Council of Latin American Studies, Mérida, Yucatán, April 4, 1988).

Horn, James J. *Cuernavaca: A Guide for Students and Tourists*. 3d ed. Brockport, N.Y.: Educational Travel Service, 1989.

Kras, Eva S. *Management in Two Cultures: Bridging the Gap between U.S. and Mexican Managers*. Yarmouth, Maine: Intercultural Press, 1989.

Lanier, Alison. *Update: Mexico*. Yarmouth, Maine: Intercultural Press, 1980.

Liebman, Seymour B. *Exploring the Latin American Mind*. Chicago: Nelson-Hall, 1976.

Lewis, Oscar. *The Children of Sánchez*. New York: Vintage Books, 1961.

Lowenthal, Abraham F. *La convivencia imperfecta: Los Estados Unidos y America Latina*. Mexico City: Editorial Patria, 1989.

Mastretta, Angeles. *Arráncame la vida*. Mexico City: Cal y Arena, 1985.

_____. *Mujeres de ojos grandes*. Mexico City: Cal y Arena, 1991.

Mendieta y Núñez, Lucio. *México indígena*. Mexico City: Editorial Porrúa, 1986.

Mexico. Amsterdam: Time-Life Books, 1985.

Meyer, Michael C., and William L. Sherman. *The Course of Mexican History*, 4th Ed. New York: Oxford University Press, 1992.

Michener, James A. *Mexico*. New York: Random House, 1992.

Morris, Mary. *Nothing to Declare: Memoirs of a Woman Traveling Alone*. New York: Penguin Books, 1988.

Nolen, Barbara, ed. *Mexico is People: Land of Three Cultures*. New York: Charles Scribner's Sons, 1973.

Paz, Octavio. *The Labyrinth of Solitude: Life and Thought in Mexico*. Trans. Lysander Kemp. New York: Grove Press, 1961.

Purcell, Susan Kaufman, ed. *Mexico in Transition: Implications for U.S. Policy*. New York: Council on Foreign Relations, 1988.

Ramos, Samuel. *Profile of Man and Culture in Mexico*. Trans. Peter G. Earle. Austin: University of Texas Press, 1962.

Riding, Alan. *Distant Neighbors: A Portrait of the Mexicans.* New York: Alfred A. Knopf, 1985.

Ross, Corrine. *Christmas in Mexico.* Lincolnwood, Ill.: Passport Books, 1991.

Smith, Peter. *Labyrinths of Power: Political Recruitment in Twentieth Century Mexico.* Princeton, N.J.: Princeton University Press, 1979.

Vázquez, Josefina Zoraida, and Meyer, Lorenzo. *The United States and Mexico. The United States in the World: Foreign Perspectives.* Chicago and London: University of Chicago Press, 1985.

Villegas, Daniel Cosío, *et al. A Compact History of Mexico.* 2d English ed. Mexico City: El Colegio de México, 1985.

Zanger, Virginia Vogel. *Exploracíon intercultural: Una guía para el estudiante.* Rowley, Mass.: Newbury House, 1984.

ABOUT THE AUTHOR

Paula R. Heusinkveld has traveled extensively in Mexico since 1965 as a student, professor, writer, lecturer, and study program director. She received her M. A. and Ph. D. in Spanish from the University of Wisconsin, with a specialty in modern Mexican literature. Currently an Associate Professor of Spanish and French at Clemson University, she has directed Clemson's summer study program in Mexico since 1984. Dr. Heusinkveld has published articles and presented numerous seminars and lectures on topics related to cross-cultural themes, foreign language learning and Latin American literature.

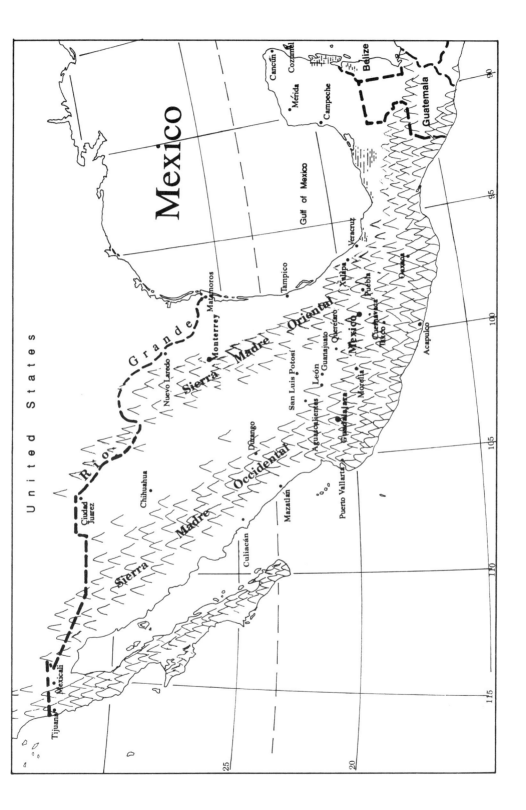